The Unauthorized Guide to SNOOPY™ COLLECTIBLES

WITH VALUES

JAN LINDENBERGER

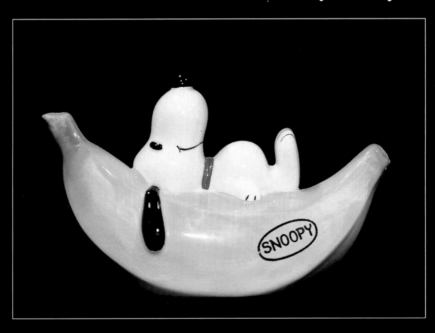

Revised Price Guide

4880 Lower Valley Rd. Atglen, PA 19310 USA

Santa Snoopy cotton pillow. F.C.I. 1980s. $5-7

Revised price guide: 1998
Copyright © 1997 by Jan Lindenberger
Library of Congress Catalog Card Number: 96-71414

Designed by "Sue"

Printed in Hong Kong
ISBN: 0-7643-0524-7

Published by Schiffer Publishing Ltd.
4880 Lower Valley Road
Atglen, PA 19310
Phone: (610) 593-1777; Fax: (610) 593-2002
E-mail: schifferbk@aol.com
Please write for a free catalog.
This book may be purchased from the publisher.
Please include $3.95 for shipping.
Try your bookstore first.

We are interested in hearing from authors
with book ideas on related subjects.

CONTENTS

ACKNOWLEDGMENTS

I wish to give a very special thank you to Cher Porges and her family. Without Cher this guide to Snoopy collectibles would not have been possible. We worked many weeks and long hours to give this project the value it deserves. Her patience in arranging and rearranging her vast collection was greatly appreciated. Along the way she found things she had forgotten were there. The information for this price guide came from her years of knowledge and research.

Between diet sodas and mustard pretzels and the privilege of me sleeping near "The Snoopy Room," *Snoopy Collectibles* was born. With the large collection it turned out to be, we felt it warranted two books, *Snoopy Collectibles* and *More Snoopy Collectibles*. Then it hit Cher that The Peanuts Gang needed its own books as well. So be it.

This meant longer hours, more days, and more diet soda. But the end result will be four much needed all color, information and price guides. Mrs. Porges didn't mind the extra work as this gives everyone's Snoopy and Peanuts collection an up-to-date price guide.

Again thanks Cher, it was wonderful working with you and I have gained you and your family as my valued friends. That's the best part of this job.

Thanks also to;

Laurel Sherry from New Holstein, Wisconsin. Laurel is the show promoter for the Mid West Snoopy Swap Meet. Her patience in allowing me to photograph on show day was greatly appreciated, as was her encouragement to do this book. Thanks too to all the dealers at the show who let me photograph their Snoopys. For information about the Snoopy Swap Meet contact Laurel by phone or fax at 414-898-5578.

Nancy Wilke, Chesterfield, Missouri. Nancy gave Cher and I a days worth of hard work and spent many hours on the phone with Cher giving us valuable information. Thanks, Nancy.

Warren Chamberlin. Mishawauka, Indiana.
Kevin Knauer, Colorado Springs, Colorado
Joel Martone, Colorado Springs, Colorado

Thank you,
Jan Lindenberger

Cher Porges resides in Fenton, Missouri, with her husband Tony and two children, Drew and Concetta. Also sharing her home are two beagles named Joe Cool and Woodstock 2. She is a more than avid collector of Snoopy. Cher has been collecting this wonderful beagle most of her life. Her home is surrounded with "Snoopy" memorabilia, Woodstock and The Peanuts gang, amounting to well over 5000 items.

Her "special" room is her get away and "off limits" to tiny hands of children and happily swaying dog tails. A bed sits in the middle of the room loaded with that white beagle and his siblings. From cotton to velour to stuffed plush. No space is left on the walls for any more pictures and some of her rare advertising posters reach to the ceiling. Shelving all around the room is filled with bobbing head dolls, ceramic figurines, music boxes, toys, Avon, puzzles, games and more. Her dressers are stuffed with Peanuts and Snoopy linen and clothing. A large plastic Snoopy toy box sits in the corner and is filled with stuffed beagles. Snoopy and the Peanuts gang hooked rugs are layered on the floor.

She welcomes you to see her fabulous collection but you must duck when entering "the room" as Snoopy chimes and wall hangers hang from the ceiling. This is a well put together room and quite full but Cher will always find room for one more treasure. It was a great pleasure to meet and work with Cher and her family. She made me quite welcome in her home.

INTRODUCTION

The beagle came into the world on October, 1950, in a comic strip named "Peanuts," created by Charles Monroe Schulz. This illustrious beagle's name is, of course, Snoopy!

Charles Schulz's uncle gave him the nickname Sparky at the tender age of 2 days in 1922, after "Spark Plug," a horse featured in Barney Google comics. This would prove prophetic. As Schulz was growing up in St. Paul, Minnesota, he would savor all the comics he could obtain, dreaming that his own artwork would be published someday.

After learning his craft through a mail order art school, he began his career as a teacher for that same school. He went to New York in 1950 to seek publication of his comic strip "Lil Folks" with United Features Syndicate. While the Syndicate liked Schulz's characters, they did not care for the name and soon changed it to "Peanuts," a decision Schulz was not fond of. Some editors of the Syndicate wanted to downplay the roll of Snoopy in the strip. Luckily Schulz gave Snoopy the prominent place he deserves in his work.

People from around the world have enjoyed Snoopy's spunk, humor, and wit. Whether he is stealing Linus's blanket or manning a space capsule, playing sports with his sidekick Woodstock or just being the coolest Beagle around, he is clearly the world's favorite beagle.

The character of Snoopy has changed immensely over the years. You can tell this by his five different two-dimensional copyright dates. When Snoopy first appeared in 1950 he always walked on four feet or sat on his haunches. This was his earliest copyright date. He earned another copyright date in 1956 when he was shown dancing on two feet with his head high. He was walking on two feet all the time by 1958, thus earning his third copyright date. His fourth copyright date came in 1965, with his ears tucked under his aviators hat and goggles covering his eyes, he began his battles as the Flying Ace, against the Red Baron. His final copyright date came in 1971, when Joe Cool appeared on the scene. Through all these changes he kept his loveable personality. (*Note: The copyright dates on the item does not reflect the year of manufacturing, only the year when the character on the piece was originally created. Thus, a piece with a 1965 copyright date may have been manufactured 1965 through today.*)

In the comic strip Charlie Brown retrieved Snoopy from The Daisy Hill Puppy farm. This white beagle had a brother named Spike who lived in Needles, California. Snoopy's other siblings were Andy, Marbles, Belle, and Olaf, otherwise known as The Daisy Hill Puppies.

According to an article by Jim Fleming, for *Boomer Magazine*, April, 1995, Mr. Schulz's comic strip has appeared in over 2,510 papers in 68 countries. By the late 1980s Peanuts was licensed to over 300 companies in 30 countries.

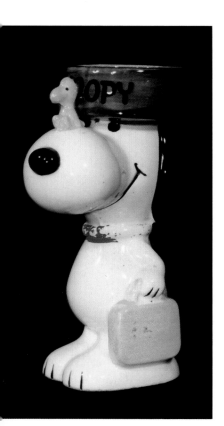

The best place to buy Snoopy and Peanuts-related items, by far, is the Mid West Snoopy Swap meet. This show and sale is put on by Laurel Sherry. One may contact Laurel at 1723 Monroe St. New Holstein, Wisconsin. 53061 for information on the next meet. Please enclose a self-addressed stamped envelop. Phone/fax 414-898-5578.

Several hundred people, who love Snoopy, get together to buy, sell, trade, and talk Snoopy. You will find Snoopy and the Peanuts gang in abundance. The prices are more than fair and the spirit among the sellers is very cheerful. To the collector it's better than Christmas. You can tell they all love that beagle!

Searching for the beagle is fun and challenging. While waiting for the next Snoopy swap meet, a good way to start a collection is to scour garage sales and flea markets. The prices are usually negotiable, but the merchandise isn't always mint. The more flaws the less you should have to pay.

Antique Malls can also be fruitful. Prices are extremely variable, but depending on condition and how knowledgeable the seller is, merchandise can be had at reasonable prices. If the item catches your eye and you have to have it, it's quite convenient to purchase it at the mall or antique shop. Remember the old slogan, "You snooze, you loose"? Purchase it when you see it or it may not be there when you go back.

If you have a bit more cash, toy shows are wonderful. Prices can be negotiated slightly and merchandise is generally in good condition. There are also several toy magazines which have advertisements from all over the country. This is a good way to track down hard to find treasures.

For new items a good source, especially around the holiday season when special things come available, is Knott's Berry Farms, Camp Snoopy.

Whatever path you choose to take in your search for Snoopy, remember the real search is for fun! I hope you enjoy this Snoopy information and price guide, and look forward to future works already in progress.

Prices may vary according to area, availability and condition. This guide offers relative values and is useful in setting a general range. Please take it with you on your "Snoopy search" and happy hunting!

Ceramic salt and pepper set. Determined. Late 1970s. 3.5" and 4.5". $45-65

Woodstock sitting on Snoopy's head, ceramic cookie jar. 1990. Willitts. $100-125

Ceramic jam jar. Late 1970s. Determined. 4.25". $30-40

Ceramic chef cookie jars. Determined. Late 1970s. 7.5" $40-50. 11" $70-80

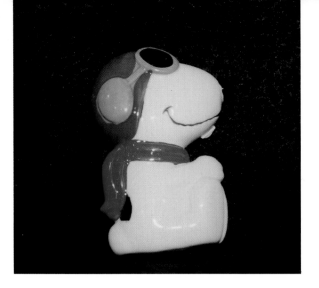

Ceramic Snoopy Flying Ace magnet. "Benjamin and Medwin Co." 1990s. $2-3

Ceramic cookie jar, $40-50. Salt and pepper set, $12-18. Magnets, $6-10. Benjamin and Medwin. 1994. Doghouse ceramics.

Ceramic Flying Ace cookie jar. Benjamin and Medwin. 1994. $40-50

Ceramic kitchen set. Benjamin and Medwin ceramics. 1993. Napkin holder, $18-22. Salt and pepper set, $12-18. Cookie jar, $40-50. Tool holder, $18-22

Two glass goodies jars. Anchor Hocking. Late 1970s. $7-12 each

Three-piece glass goodies jars. Anchor Hocking. Late 1970s. 5.5", $7-9; 6.5", $8-10; 8.5", $10-12

Glass cookie jar. Snoopy eating cookies painted on front. Anchor Hocking. 1990s. $25-35

Decanter for juice. Anchor Hocking. 1980s. $12-17

Glass juice jug. $12-17

Juice set with decanter and glasses. Anchor Hocking. $18-23

Tsukuba, Japan, Expo '85 drinking glass.
$20-25

Political Snoopy drinking glasses. 1970s. $5-7
each

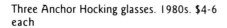

Three Anchor Hocking glasses. 1980s. $4-6
each

Anchor Hocking Snoopy root beer Hocking
mug. Early 1980s. 7.75" high. Heavy. $18-23

Snoopy drinking glasses from Welsh's Jelly.
1980s. $3-5 each.

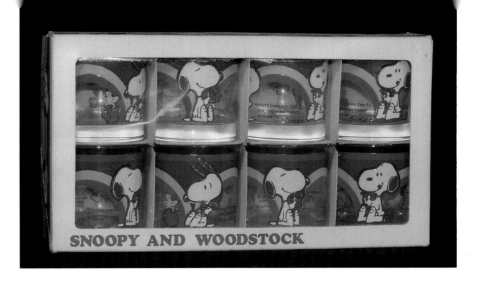

Set of 8 glasses. Anchor Hocking. 1980s.
$20-30

Snoopy drinking glass. Denz, Japan. 1990s.
$10-12

Glass Anchor Hocking political coffee cups.
1970s. $6-8 each

Four stoneware coffee cups. Taylor International. 1970s. $8-12 each

Ceramic Snoopy chauffeur coffee cup. 1980s.
$8-12

Snoopy in tux and top hat, ceramic coffee cup.
Determined. Mid-1970s. $10-15

Front and back view of ceramic Joe Cool stein by
Determined, 1970s. $30-40

Ceramic Snoopy "Rah" stein from Determined. 1970s. $20-30

Cowboy and sailing Snoopy, plastic children's cups. $6-8

Plastic cup given by Knott's Berry Farm. 1990s. Given with children's meal or birthday party. $1-2

Plastic cups. 1980s. $5-7

China dish set. Plates, cup and saucer, tea cup,
tea pot, bowl. Japan. 1990s. $120-150

Plastic 4 piece dinner set. Danara. Late
1980s-early 1990s. $15-20

Snoopy and Woodstock dinnerware set.
Melamine Zak Designs. 1995. $25-35

Ceramic "Snoopy Around the World" chili
bowls. Determined. 1970s. $15-25

Ceramic chili bowl, "Come and get it!"
Determined. 1970s. $15-25

Pewter teaspoon with Snoopy in
Beagle Scout outfit, from Knott's,
Camp Snoopy. 1990s. $5-7

Plastic handle children's flatware. Pecoware.
1990s. $7-10

Stainless steel baby spoon. Determined. 1980s.
$3-5

Snoopy and Woodstock plastic condiment server, 1980s. $4-5.

Oil cloth apron. Early 1980s. $15-20

Melmac spoon rest. Yee Cheong Melamine ware. 1990s. $8-12

Oil cloth Snoopy apron. 1980s. $15-20

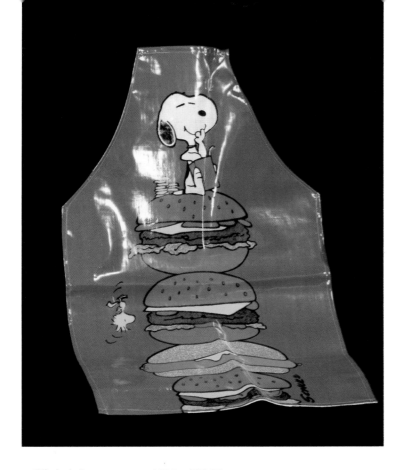

Oil cloth Snoopy apron. 1980s. $15-20

Cotton party apron from Chex cereal. 1980s. Child's: $15-20; adult's: $20-25

Cotton apron and hat. 1980s. $12-18

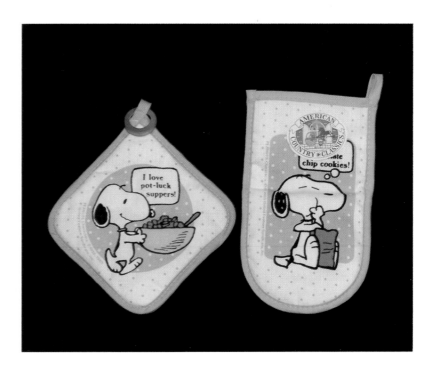

Cotton hot pot holders. 1990s. $4-6 each

Tin canister set. The tins nest within each
other. Determined. 1979. $50-75

Tin round serving tray. Determined Productions. 1979. $25-35

Snoopy on pumpkin plastic cookie cutter.
5.5" x 6.5". Hallmark. 1972. $150-250
mint in package

Plastic set of four Snoopy cookie cutters.
Hallmark. $125-150 mint in package

Plastic Snoopy cookie cutters. Hallmark. 1975. 4.5". $40-80 set mint in package.

Melmac cutting board by Brookpark. 1979. 8" x 10" with 5" handle. $25-35

Plastic Snoopy placemat. 1990s. $4-6

Water motion placemat from CTI Industries. Mid-1990s. $5-7

19

Plastic Snoopy file or recipe box. 1980s. $8-10

Paper napkins from Northern. 1980s-1990s. $2-5

Metal Snoopy recipe box. 1970s, Chein. $18-23

Paper napkins "Snoopy for President." Hallmark. 5" x 5". 1970s. $10-15

Snoopy plastic sandwich bags. Carousel products. 1980s. $4-6

Throughout the 1980s and 1990s, Conimar, the lunch bag people, produced a variety of ways to brown bag in style. $2-4 each

Snoopy with dish on his head paper lunch bag package. $2-4

Package of paper lunch bags. $2-4

Snoopy eating sandwich paper lunch bag package. $2-4

Package of Beagle paper lunch bags. $2-4

Paper lunch bag with Snoopy and Woodstock. $2-4 package

Paper lunch bag, "Flashbeagle." Conimar. 1980s. $6-8 package

Paper litter bag. "Keep America Beautiful." Conimar. 1980s. $8-12 package

Ceramic peanut dish with Snoopy laying on top. Late 1970s. Determined. 4" x 7.5", $100-125. 2.5" x 3", $70-90

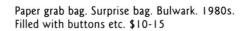

Paper grab bag. Surprise bag. Bulwark. 1980s. Filled with buttons etc. $10-15

Melmac coasters from Japan. Yee Cheong
Melamine ware. 1990s. $4-7

Plastic Flying Ace corn set. Wecolite
Co. Inc., 1980s. $5-7

Plastic Funstraws from Danara. 1980s-1990s.
$2-3

Plastic ice cream scoop from Wecolite co. Inc.
1980s. $5-7

Bag of Snoopy's Chocolate Grahams from
Famous Amos. 1990s. 2oz. $1-3. 10oz. $4-6

Snoopy and Woodstock dish. Japan. 1990s.
$10-15

Snoopy cereal box from Japan. 1994. $5-8

Snoopy's Choice frozen dinners. Con
Agra-Healthy Choice. 1989s. $4-6 each with
plastic cooking dish.

The flying Ace plastic bottle cap. One of a two
cap set on a card. Wecolite Co. 1980s-1990s.
$5-7

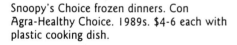

Snoopy with Woodstock foil-lined food box
from Japan. 1990s. $4-6

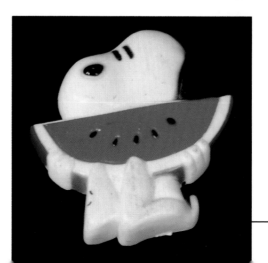

Snoopy eating watermelon
plastic magnet. Wecolite.
1980s-1990s. $5-7

Snoopy cotton reversible comforter with matching sheets. 1980s. $50-60

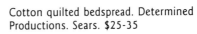

Snoopy bedspread and pillow case. 1980s. J.C. Penny. $40-50

Cotton quilted bedspread. Determined Productions. Sears. $25-35

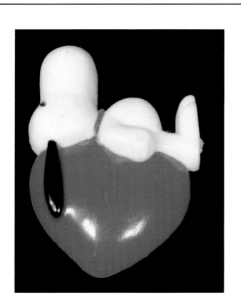

Snoopy laying on heart plastic magnet. Wecolite. 1980s-1990s. $5-7

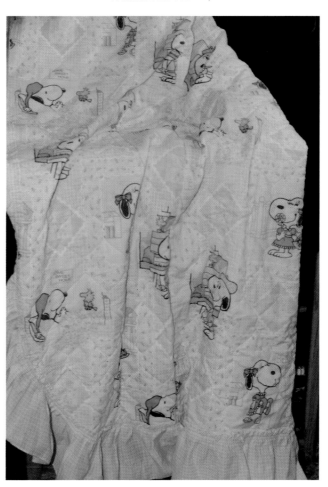

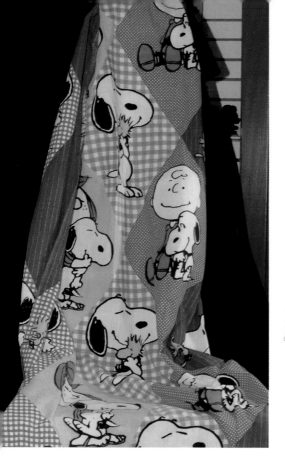

Cotton Peanuts gang sheet. 1970s. $15-20

Cotton twin sheet set. Snoopy and his bed.
1990s. $20-25

Cotton flannel sheet and pillow case. Frano.
1990s. $20-25

Cotton bedspread. 1970s. $20-25

Cotton sheet. "Love is a friend." 1970s. $15-20

Cotton/polyester drapes with laughing Snoopy.
Cannon. 1990s. $20-25

Flannel sheet set. Franco. 1980s. $20-25

Cotton Snoopy sleeping bag. 1980s. $20-25

Nylon sleeping bag. 1980s. Ero Industries. $20-30

Nylon sleeping bag with Snoopy sitting in a shoe. Ero Industries. Early 1990s. $20-30

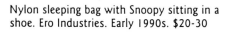

Cotton flannel "Pillow Lounger." Franco. Good Housekeeping. Late 1980s. $20-30

Nylon Snoopy sleeping bag from Ero Industries. 1990s. $20-30

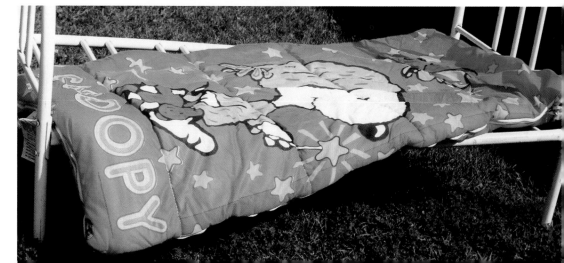

Cotton baby bunting bag/quilt. 1980s. $20-25

Terry cloth beach towel, Snoopy gone fishing. Franco. 1990s. $20-25

Cotton weave throw blanket, Hollywood Snoopy. Canon. Late 1980s. $25-30

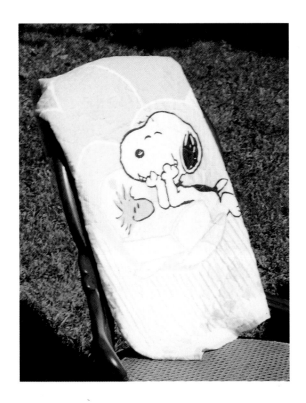

Terry cloth bath towel set. Late 1980s. $20-25

Cotton baby quilt from a kit. 1980s. F.C.I. $15-20

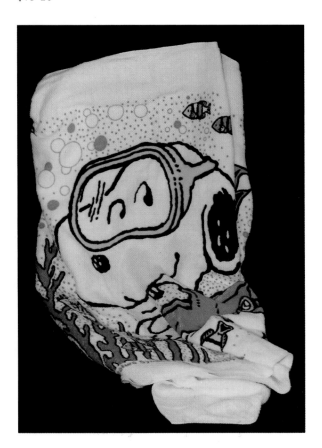

Terry cloth beach towel. Snoopy and Woodstock. 1990s. $15-20

Terry cloth beach towel. Snoopy with underwater mask. $17-22

Terry cloth Snoopy and Woodstock wash cloth. Japan. 1990s. $5-7

Terry cloth wash cloth, Snoopy taking a bath with Woodstock. Franco. 1980s. $3-5

Shower curtain and bath towel. Snoopy and Woodstock. 1990s. Curtain, $20-25. Towel, $10-15

Cotton Joe Cool pillow. Mid-1990s. Town and Country Linen Corp. 19", $15-20. 14", $9-12.

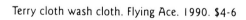

Cotton pillow toys. 1970s. $8-12

Terry cloth wash cloth. Flying Ace. 1990. $4-6

Cotton stuffed pillow. Snoopy golfer. Determined, 1971. $20-25

Green Snoopy fleece pillow. Determined. 1980s. $20-25

Cotton stuffed Snoopy pillow. Snoopy bowler. Determined, 1971. $20-25

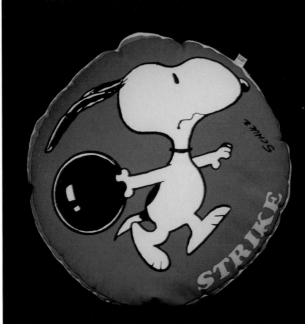

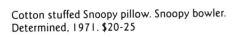

Cotton Snoopy and Woodstock pillow. Mid-1990s. Town and Country Linen Corp. $9-20

Cotton stuffed pillow. Snoopy ice hockey. Determined, 1971. $20-25

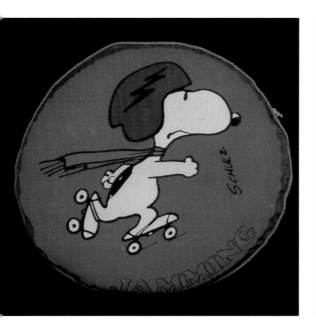

Cotton Snoopy skater pillow. Determined, 1971.
$20-25

Marshmallow Flying Ace pillow toy. 18".
Spencer Gifts Inc. 1990s. $20-25

Cotton Snoopy football pillow. Determined,
1971. $20-25

Marshmallow Snoopy with doghouse pillow toy.
18". 1990s. Spencer Gifts Inc. $20-25

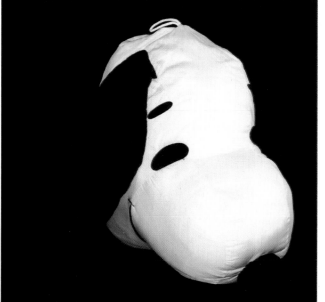

Marshmallow Snoopy head pillow toy. 26" x
20". 1990s. Spencer Gifts Inc. $20-25

Marshmallow Snoopy in doghouse pillow toy. 18". 1990s. $20-25

Throughout the 1980s F.C.I. made a huge assortment of plain and even velour-like fabric pillows. They were reasonably priced cut-and-sew project. They include quilts, pillows, charts, sheets and shoe bags, some of which are shown below. The pillows were frequently made into wall hangings and appliques. 1980s.

Cotton Charlie Brown pillow. F.C.I. 1980s. $7-9

Marshmallow Flying Ace pillow toy. 26" x 20". 1990s. Spencer Gifts Inc. $20-25

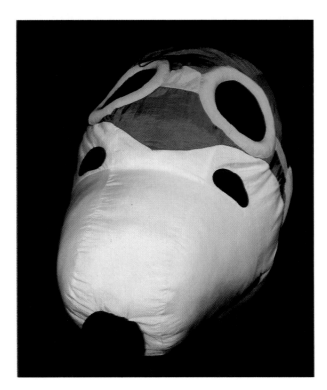

Marshmallow Flying Ace pillow toy. 26" x 20". 1990s. Spencer Gifts Inc. $20-25

Cotton Christmas Snoopy and walking Snoopy pillows. F.C.I. 1980s. $7-9.

Cotton heart-shaped, Snoopy on house, pillow. F.C.I. 1980s. $7-9

Cotton Snoopy shaped pillow. F.C.I. 1980s. $7-9

Stuffed cotton pillow. F.C.I. 1980s. $7-9

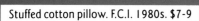

Uncut cotton Snoopy pillow. F.C.I. 1980s. $7-9

Cotton Snoopy baby pillow. F.C.I. 1980s. $7-9

Uncut Snoopy Tennis player, cotton pillow.
F.C.I. 1980s. $7-9

Uncut cotton fabric pillow. Snoopy in airplane with Woodstock. 1980s. $7-9

SNOOPY'S BATH TIME

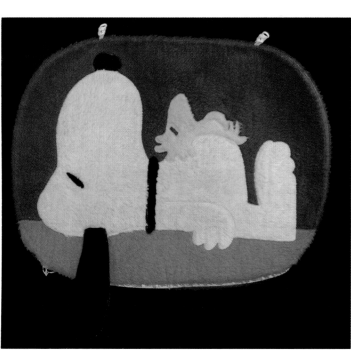

Acrylic plush pillow sham. 1980s. $15-20

Snoopy tub buddies bathtub puppets by Dragons Are Too Seldom Inc. 1990s. $8-12.

Snoopy and Woodstock bathroom rug. 1990s. $15-20

Snoopy soap dispensers. Left: Creative Specialties. 1980s. 8oz. $7-10; 16oz. $10-15. Right: Snoopy soap pump for the whole family. Determined. 1980s. $5-7

Snoopy Clean-up Set for Boys. Giftique Div. 1990. $12-15.

Snoopy bubble bath containers. Collectible characters. 1995. Minnetonka Brands Inc. $5-7 each

Snoopy and Belle talc. Creative Specialties, 1908s. $6-10

Snoopy and friends bath soap. Cosrich Inc. 1990s. $3-4

Peanuts gang soap by Creative Services Ltd.
Late 1980s. $6-10

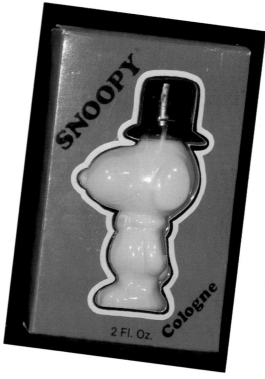

Snoopy spray cologne. Creative Specialties Ltd.
Late 1980s. $15-20

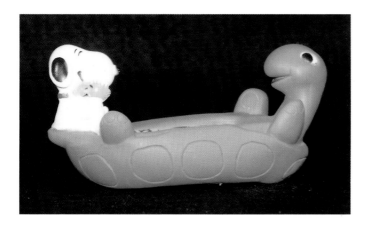

Rubber floating turtle soap dish. Wecolite Co.
1980s. $5-8

Snoopy laying on raft soap dish. Wecolite Co.
Early 1980s. $5-8

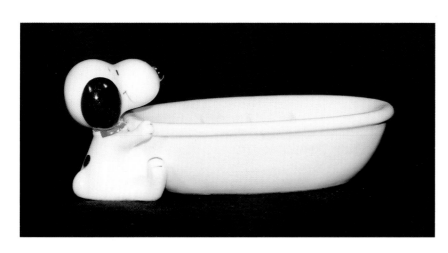

Ceramic soap dish. Determined. 1980s. $20-30

Ceramic soap dish, Snoopy swimming, Woodstock on rim. Snoopy and Co. Early 1990s. $10-15

Ceramic covered soap dish. Came in an assortment of colors. 1980s. Determined. $30-40

Ceramic container with bubble bath. Snoopy sitting in bucket of bubbles. Determined Productions. 1970s. $30-40

Ceramic Soap dish and tooth brush holder from Willitts. 1990. $50-60 for both

Complete bathroom set. Plastic waste can and accessories. Snoopy and Co. Can $20-30. Tissue holder $15-20. Ceramic cup, toothbrush holder, soap dispenser and soap dish. $7-9 each

Ceramic figurine, Snoopy sitting in bubble bath. Determined prod. 1970s. $30-40

Avon Snoopys were available from 1968-1975, making it fun for kids to wash up. Always try to obtain mint in box, as slightly loved things with no box are not as valuable.

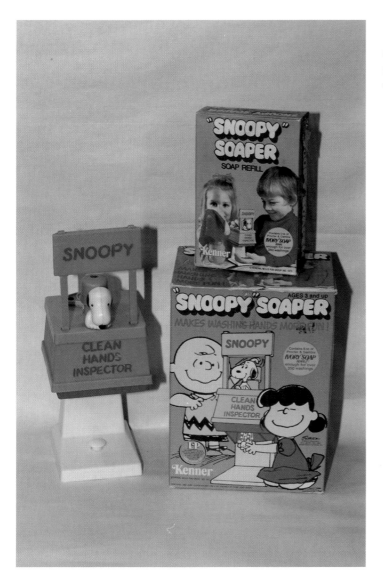

Snoopy plastic Soaper by Kenner. 1975. $35-45

Avon Snoopy Come Home plastic soap dish, came with bar of soap. 1973. $15-20

Avon floating Snoopy dish. Came with soap laying on his tummy. 1968. $15-20

Flying Ace bubble bath from Avon. 1969.
$15-20

Snoopy on skis bubble bath from Avon. 1974.
$30-40

Milk glass Flying Ace bubble bath from Avon.
1969. $15-20. Not shown: blue lid.

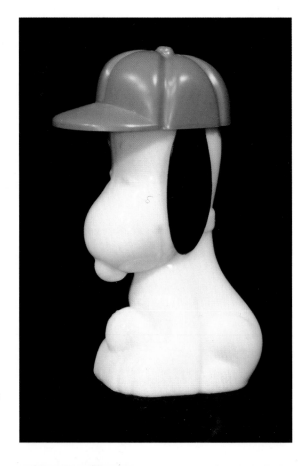

Milk glass Snoopy after shave lotion from
Avon. 1970s. $10-15

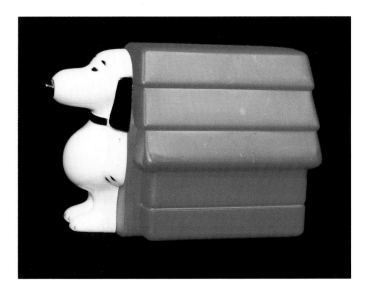

Snoopy on doghouse no-tears shampoo from Avon. 1969. $18-25

Snoopy and Woodstock mirror made in England. Late 1970s, early 1980s. $10-15

Snoopy make-up hand mirror. 11". 1970s. England. $7-10

Plastic dresser set. 1980s. $25-35

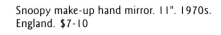

Plastic mirror. 1980s. $7-10

Snoopy mirrors made in England. Late 1970s-
early 1980s. $10-15

Snoopy mirror back. "What a face". England,
1970s. $10-15

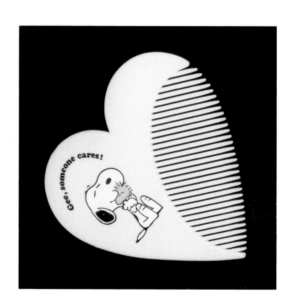

Plastic heart shaped-comb. Japan. 1990s. $4-6

Plastic Snoopy brush and comb set from Avon.
1970. $15-20

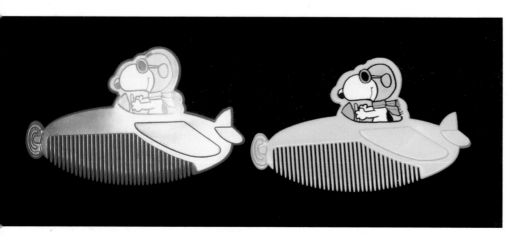

Plastic Flying Ace airplane-shaped combs.
1990s. Japan. $4-6 each

Plastic ice cream cone-shaped comb. 1990s.
Japan. $4-6

Plastic Snoopy toothbrush. $15-20

Retractable plastic hair brush. 6.5". 1990s. $7-10

Plastic Snoopy tooth brush set. Determined. 1980s. $20-25. Press tooth brush and he brushes his teeth with you.

Snoopy toothbrushes. Oral-B. 1980s. $4-5 each

Plastic battery operated toothbrush by Kenner. 1972. $45-55

ITT, International Trading Technology, produced a wide variety of plastic and die cast toys in the late 1980s and 1990s.

Snoopy Brush-Brush Toothbrush. ITT. 1990s. $15-20

Plastic cup and toothbrush holder. Pecoware. 1990s. $15-20

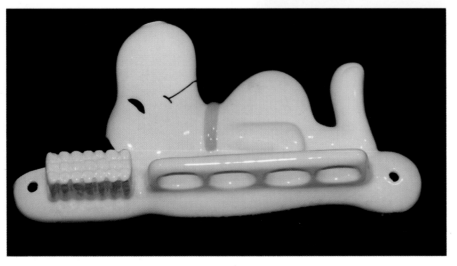

China tooth brush holder. Determined. 1980s. 7.25" x 4", $75-100

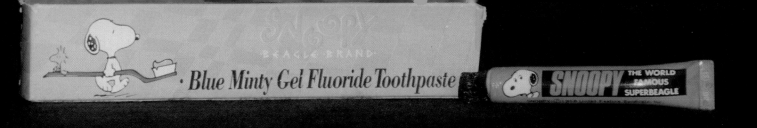

Snoopy fluoride toothpaste. $4-6

Snoopy bandages. $2-3 each

Snoopy bandages. 1980s. Quantasia. $3-4 each

Fabric arm sling. Quantasia, 1980s. $7-10

Snoopy nail polish. 1990s. $7-10. These came in various colors and pins of all the Peanut characters.

Snoopy make up brush by Determined
Productions. 1990s. Japan. $5-7

Plastic smoke detector. Jameson. Late
1980s-early 90s. $25-35

Paper cup holder with paper cups. Dixie. 1980s.
Cup dispenser in box. $15-20.

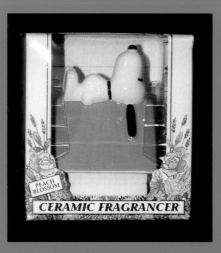

Snoopy paper refill cups from Dixie. 1980s. $7-12

Ceramic fragrancer. Hand made and hand painted in the United Kingdom. 1990s. Yellow, orange or purple. $30-40

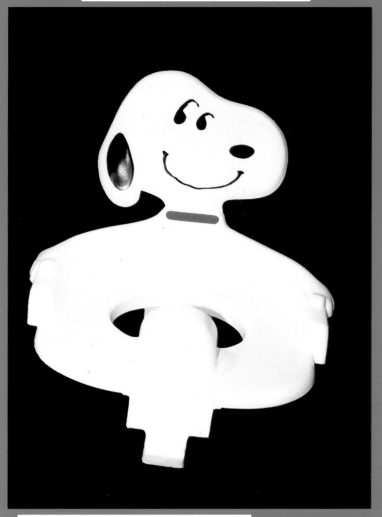

Plastic baby potty training seat. Knickerbocker. 1980s. $10-15

SNOOPY'S TOY ROOM

Aviva made a large variety of Snoopy and the Gang toys in wood, plastic, and die-cast. It was a great loss when they went out of business in the early 1980s.

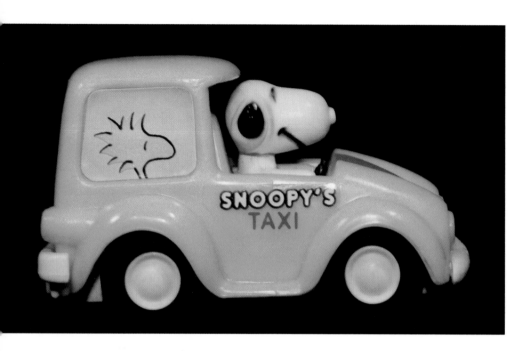

Snoopy's plastic taxi from Aviva. 1980s. $6-10

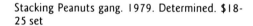

Stacking Peanuts gang. 1979. Determined. $18-25 set

International Trading Technology (ITT) plastic Snoopy on skateboard. 2.5". 1990s. $3-5

Plastic Snoopys and Charlie Brown sitting in
wagons. Aviva. 1977. $15-20 each

Plastic Snoopys on metal skateboards from
Aviva. 1980s. $15-20

Plastic Snoopy and Woodstock on skateboards
from Aviva. Late 1970s. $15-18

Plastic Snoopy on motorcycle by Aviva. Early
1980s. $10-15

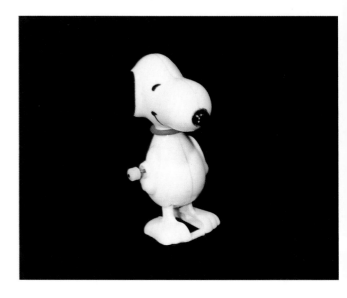

Plastic wind up walking Snoopy from Aviva.
Mid-1970s. $3-6

Aviva metal Joe cool wagon. (Handle missing.)
1977. $15-20

Plastic wind up Snoopy walker from Aviva.
1975. $5-9

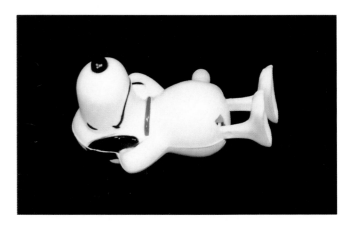

Plastic wind up swimming Snoopy. Unknown
manufacturer and year. $3-5

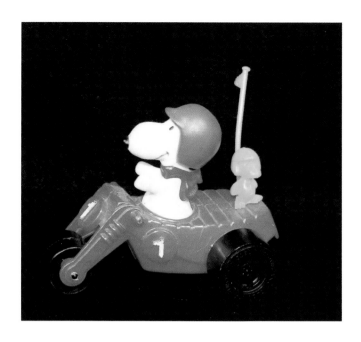

Plastic Snoopy and Woodstock on Hot Rod.
Child Guidance. 1970s. $10-15

Die cast Snoopy Towing truck from Hasbro.
1980s. $5-10

Scout guide on bus by Hasbro. 1990s. $5-10

BOIS MASSIF LAQUE vilac

Wood Snoopy in race car from France. Vilac. 1990s. $20-30

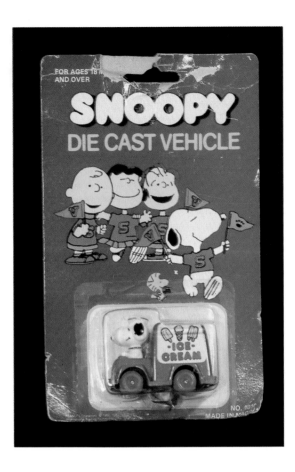

Snoopy die cast Ice Cream truck. ITT. Late 1980s-early 1990s. $8-15

ITT made many various plastic action toys. Late 1980s-early 1990s. Snoopy on bike. $10-15. Not pictured Woodstock on bike. $10-15

Snoopy plastic Carrying Case Garage. Late 1980s-early 1990s. ITT. $20-25

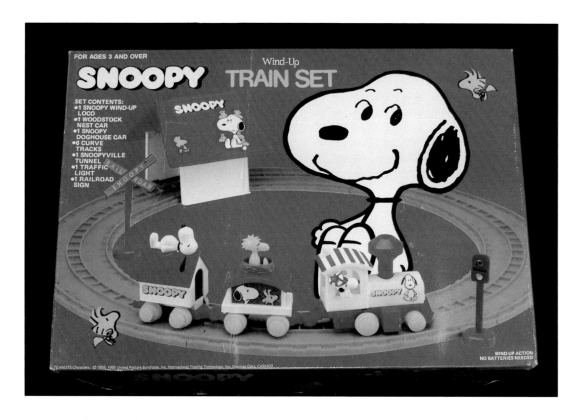

Snoopy plastic Wind-Up Train Set. Sold as set or individual train. ITT. 1990s. Set, $20-30. Train, $10-15

Plastic Snoopy 3-piece train. ITT, 1990s. $10-15

Large Snoopy die cast car and airplane from ITT. Average length 4.5". 1990s. $10-15

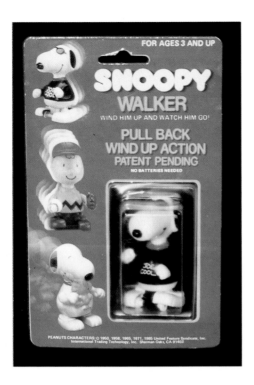

Plastic Snoopy Walker. ITT. 1990s. $4-7

Plastic Snoopy musical guitar. Mattel. Late 1960s. $25-35

Metal "Snoopy in the Music Box" by Mattel. 1969. $25-45

Joe Cool skateboard. Nash Manufacturing. 1980s-1990s. $45-55. Not shown are some that came with handles to use also as scooter.

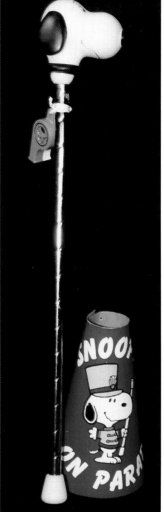

Snoopy on parade, drum majorette and cheerleading set. Synergistics. 1982. Not shown: blue pom-poms. $40-50

Knott's Berry Farm plastic yo-yo. $10-15

Plastic Snoopy Hummingbird Yo-Yo from Hallmark. 1976. $30-40

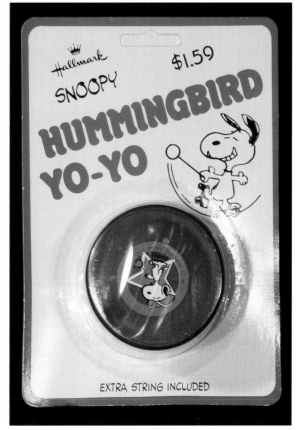

Metal tambourine with Woodstock. 1970s.
$20-30

Metal drum with Snoopy as the leader. 1970s.
$60-75

Metal megaphone with plastic insert by Chein and Co. 1970s. Beneath the picture are the stars of the movie "A Boy Named Charlie Brown." $20-30. Came in various colors.

Plastic spinning top from Ohio Art. 1980s. $15-20

Tin Snoopy & the Gang toy top. Ohio Art. 1980s. $10-15

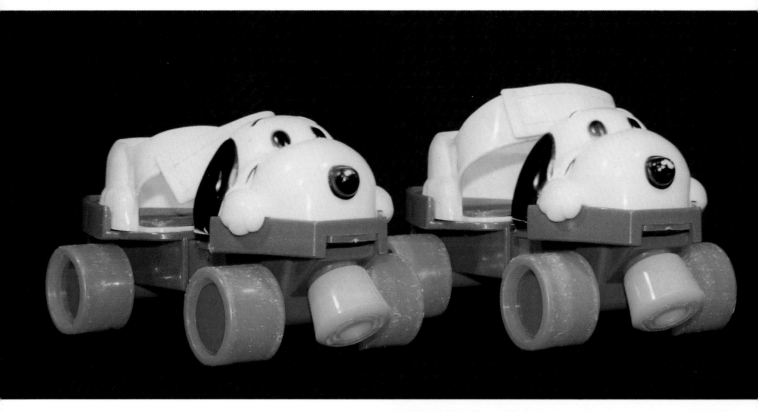

Plastic Snoopy shaped roller skates. Nash
Manufacture. 1980s. $25-35

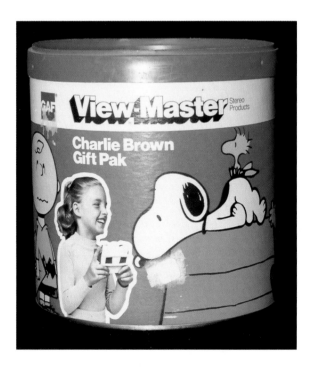

Charlie Brown deluxe Gift Pak View-Master
from GAF. Late 1970s. $40-50

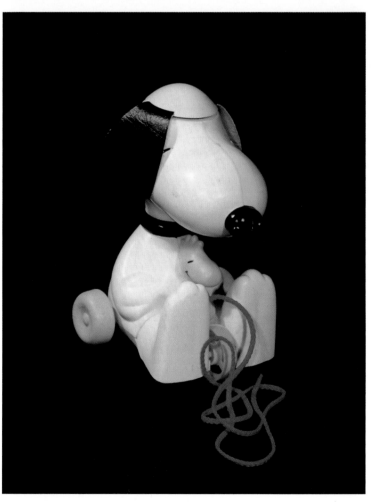

Plastic Snoopy holding Woodstock, pull toy.
Snoopy's ears twirl. Romper Room/Hasbro.
1980s. $10-25

Romper Room plastic Snoopy Counting Camera
by Hasbro. Pull Snoopy's tail to count. 1980s.
$10-15

Plastic Snoopy goes in and out of doghouse
when the crank in the back is turned. Missing
Woodstock, which also moves. 1980s. Romper
Room/Hasbro. $20-30

Romper Room plastic, twirling, Snoopy play
phone by Hasbro. 1980s. $10-20

Rubber Belle and Snoopy dolls with plush ears
by Determined. 1982. $40-60 each in box. Not
shown: Snoopy in tuxedo, tennis outfit,
walking with Walkman, golfer, sailor,
rollerskater, jogger, Belle walking with
Walkman, and as a bride.

Rubber Snoopy collector doll. The soccer player
from Determined Productions. 8". 1982. $40-60

Rubber Snoopy Tub-Time toy by Knickerbocker.
1980s. $25-35

Rubber "Dress Me" Snoopy and "Dress Me"
Belle dolls by Knickerbocker. 1983. 7.5". $30-50
each in box. Outfits were sold separately.
$15-20 mint on card

Jointed rubber Snoopy Astronaut with Woodstock. Knickerbocker. 1979. $35-45

Plastic Snoopy scoutmaster toy. Made up of 6 stack up pieces to take apart and put together. 5.5" x 9". Romper Room/ Hasbro. 1980s. $20-30

Plastic Snap Tite model kit is Joe Cool. Snoopy can ride the waves and spin. Monogram/Mattel. $60-75

Snoopy Astronaut in original box by Determined Productions. 1960s. $80-110

Snoopy Kaleidoscope. 1980s. $30-40

Plastic mini gumball dispenser. Late 1980s. Superior Toy Co. $8-12

Plastic wind up toys. The champ, the drummer, and the chef. 1977. $30-40

Plastic Joe Cool and Woodstock gumball machine. 1990s. Super Toy Mfg. $20-30

Die cast Flying Ace plane. "Aviva". 4 3/4". 1977. $18-30. Not shown in this series: Snoopy family car w/Linus, Charlie, Woodstock; Snoopy sports car; Snoopy racer; Snoopy locomotive; Snoopy fire engine. $25-35 each.

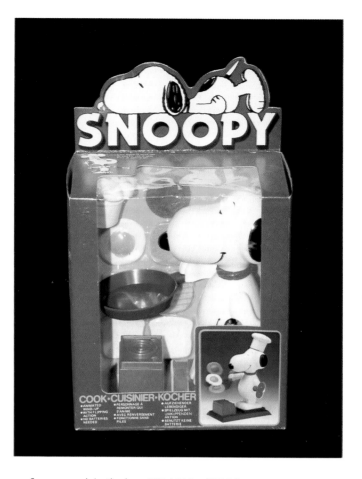

Snoopy cook in the box. ITT. 1990s. $15-20

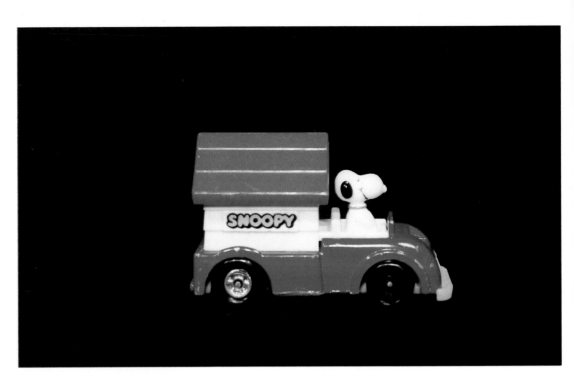

Mini die-cast Snoopy driving truck with doghouse on back from Aviva. 1977. $8-15

Mini die cast cat catcher vehicle. 2.5". "Aviva" 1977. $7-15. This well-loved die cast toy is an example of many mini die cast vehicles produced in the 1970s/1980s. $8-15

Mini die-cast Snoopy hay truck. Aviva. 1977. $8-15

Snoopy fun figures in different poses. From Comic Spain. These unique fun figures came in 22 poses plus 11 with Snoopy carrying various flags. 1990s. $8-12.

Snoopy golfer and Snoopy cowboy PVC fun figures. 1990s. $5-8

Snoopy fun figures. 1980s. $5-8

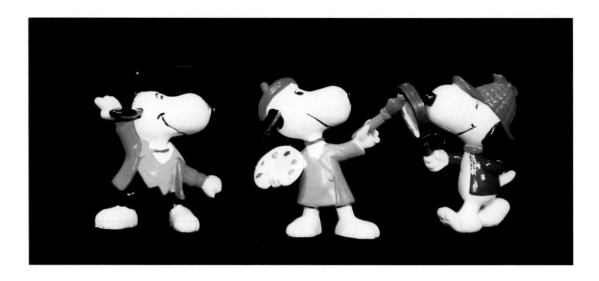

Snoopy fun figures. 1980s. $5-8

Snoopy fun figures. 1980s-1990s. $5-8

Snoopy with cake 1990 and Snoopy chef
1980s, party series. $5-8

40th anniversary Snoopy fun figure set by Applause. 1990. $20-30

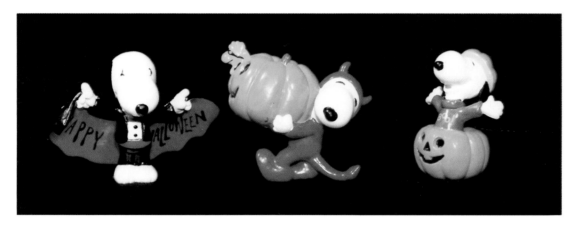

Snoopy Halloween fun figures. 1990s. $5-8 each

SNOOPY'S GAMEWORLD: PUZZLES AND FUN STUFF

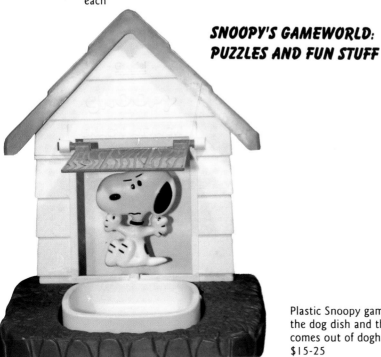

Comic strip card game. U.S. Game Systems. 1995. $8-12

Plastic Snoopy game. Remove the bones from the dog dish and the door lifts up and Snoopy comes out of doghouse. Gabriel. 1980s. $15-25

Battery operated plastic Snoopy Speedway
from Aviva. Late 1970s. $100-150. Various
raceways, train sets, etc. were also produced.

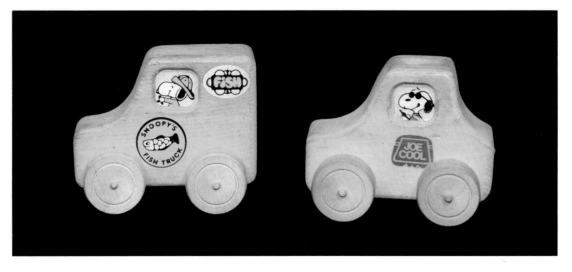

Wooden vehicles from Aviva. Snoopy's fish
truck and Joe Cool car. Not shown: Flying Ace
Snoopy in Volkswagen Bug, Snoopy's Farm Truck,
and Snoopy and Woodstock in a car. 1977. $25-35

Plastic My Pal Snoopy game. Pull his arm and
he throws the ball. Romper Room/Hasbro.
1980. In 1979 it was called Snoopy, My Friend.
$35-40

Lionel Snoopy and Woodstock Handcar.
$125-175. Not shown: Lucy and Charlie Brown
Hand Car. $125-175

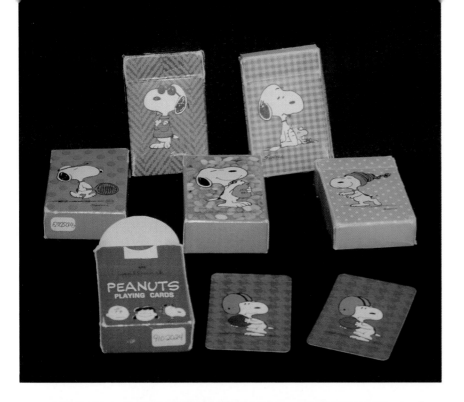

Decks of mini card games, early 1970s.
Hallmark. 2.5" x 1.75". If unopened gold seal on
top: $10-15

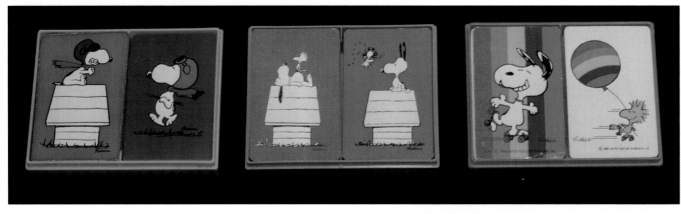

Assorted double decks of playing cards from
Hallmark. Mid-1970s. $25-35 each

Snoopy playing cards. U.S. Games Systems Inc.
1995. $6-9

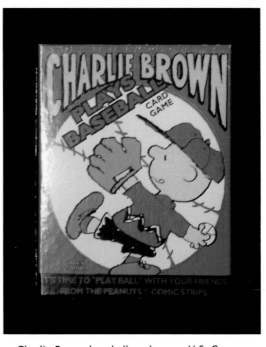

Charlie Brown baseball card game. U.S. Game
Systems. 1995. $10-15

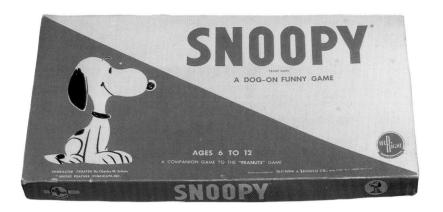

Snoopy: A Dog-on Funny Game from Selright.
Selchow and Richter. 1960s. $25-35

Snoopy Come Home Game from Milton Bradley.
Determined Productions. 1975. $18-25

Snoopy's Doghouse Game from Milton Bradley.
1977. $30-40

Snoopy and the Red Baron action game. Milton
Bradley. Determined Productions. Early 1970s.
$15-25

Snoopy Card Game by Milton Bradley. Determined Productions. Mid-1970s. $18-25

Snoopy Ball Darts. Totally safe game.
Synergistics Research Corp. Not shown: Roller
Derby and Snoopy on target. Determined
Productions. 1978. $20-25

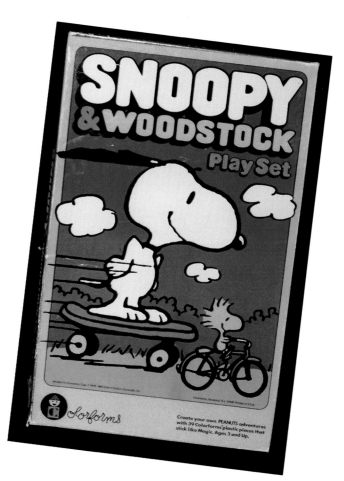

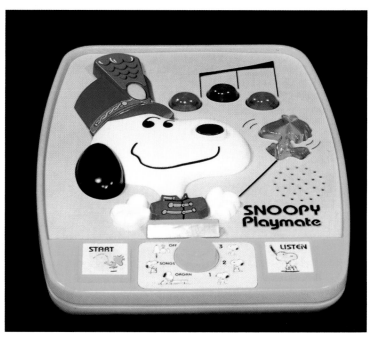

Plastic electronic Snoopy playmate toy. Romper Room/Hasbro. 1980. $110-150

Snoopy & Woodstock Play Set by Colorforms. 1970s-1980s. $15-20

Mini Colorforms play set. Butterfly. 1980s. $4-6

Snoopy & Belle Colorforms Dress Up Set from Colorforms. 1970s-1980s. $15-20

SNOOPY and his friends!

ACRYLIC PAINT by NUMBER SET

PAINTS DRY IN MINUTES

BRUSH CLEANS WITH WATER

new easy open container

4072 Time for Lunch

4072 Be a Friend

FOR AGES 8 TO ADULT

FRAMES NOT INCLUDED

TWO 8"x10" PANELS ∙ 8 COLORS ∙ BRUSH AND INSTRUCTIONS

Another DETERMINED Production

PEANUTS Characters: Copr. © 1950, 1958, 1965 United Feature Syndicate, Inc.

...ber set. In the early 1980s, Determined Productions
...paint by number sets. Selections included painting
...k velvet and cardboard panels, and even a wooden
...ament set. $8-15; ornament kit $25-35

Peanuts Trace and Color book by Saalfield. Late 1960s. $20-30

Four puzzles in one, Snoopy and Woodstock from Springbrook. Mid-1990s. $10-15

Interlocking puzzle with Snoopy and Woodstock from Hallmark. 1990s. $10-15.

"Braces make beautiful faces!" Snoopy puzzle. Springbrook by Hallmark. 1980s. 7" x 10.5". $5-8

Sun bathing Snoopy and Woodstock puzzle
from Milton Bradley. Late 1970s. $8-12

Cardboard Snoopy puzzle. Milton Bradley.
1980s-1990s. $5-8

1000 piece puzzle, "Dog of 1000 Faces" from
Springbrook. Late 1980s. $15-20.

Cardboard puzzle Snoopy and Woodstock's
family from Milton Bradley. 1980s-1990s. $3-6

Cardboard puzzle Snoopy in the rain from
Milton Bradley. 1980s-1990s. $3-6

Cardboard puzzle Snoopy and Woodstock.
11" x 14". Milton Bradley. 1980s-1990s. $3-6

Cardboard puzzle Snoopy fishing with
Woodstock from Milton Bradley. 1980s-1990s. $3-6

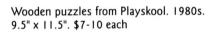

Wooden puzzles from Playskool. 1980s.
9.5" x 11.5". $7-10 each

Snoopy and Charlie Brown wooden puzzle.
9.5" x 11.5". 1980s. $10-15

Wooden puzzle from Playskool. Snoopy on dog
house. 9.5" x 11.5". 1980s. $10-15

Metal round waste can with plastic roof/lid.
Chein. Early 1970s. 16". $25-45

Vinyl Snoopy mini chair. Determined. 1970s.
$10-15

Special edition Knott's Camp Snoopy Kodak
110 camera. Snoopy's Snapshot. Mid-1990s.
$25-35

Metal Snoopy harp. Trophy Music Co.
1969-1970. No markings on the harp.
$15-20 in the box

Plastic Snoopy Fun Flashlight from Garrity.
Suction cup/non-refillable. Early 1990s. $6-10

Metal waste can with graduate Snoopy. Chein. 1970s. 13". Opposite side is Charlie Brown reading report card. "Good Grief". $20-40

Waste paper can/stool. "Let's Party." 1980s. $25-45

Plastic Snoopy in doghouse toy box. 1980s. 22" x 18". $40-50

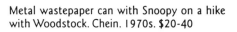

Metal wastepaper can with Snoopy on a hike with Woodstock. Chein. 1970s. $20-40

Plastic Snoopy Step Stool. Knickerbocker.
1980s. $10-15

Rubber mat for playing pogs. 1990s. $7-11

Rubber mat for playing pogs. 1990s. $7-11

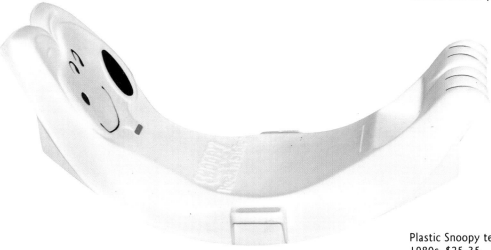

Plastic Snoopy teeter totter. Knickerbocker.
1980s. $25-35.

Joe Cool storage box. 15.5" 1988. Trojan
Luggage Company. $40-50

Best of Friends storage box. 15.5". 1988. Trojan
Luggage Company. $40-50

Flying Ace storage box. 15.5". 1988. Trojan
Luggage Company. $40-50

A Beagle for All Seasons storage box. 15.5".
1988. Trojan Luggage Company. $40-50

Plush Snoopy rocking dog on a wooden base.
1990s. Unknown maker. $225-250

Snoopy ceiling fan. All seasons design. Sisco.
1980s. $100-125

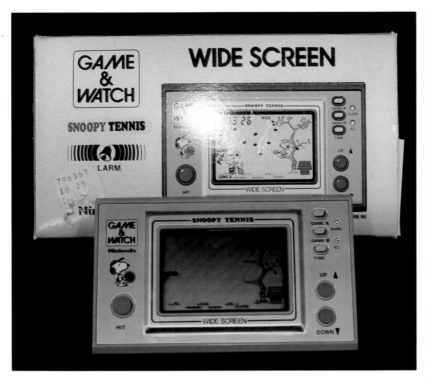

Tennis Game and watch combination, wide screen by Nintendo. 1980s. 4.5" x 2.5". $60-90

SNOOPY'S PLUSHLAND: PUPPETS AND CLOTH BEAGLES

Snoopy puppet from Pelham Puppets, England. 8". 1979. $-40-60

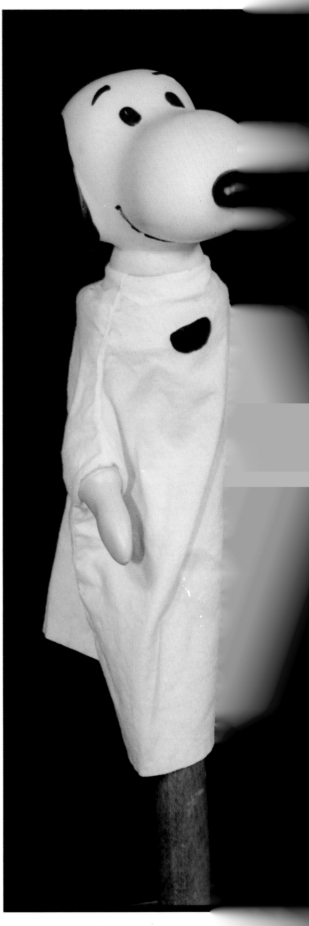

Snoopy hand puppet with rubber head body. 1980s. $50-75

Plush Snoopy puppet, Paw Pets, Applause. 1990s. $25-35

Peanuts Magic Catch Puppets. Synergistics
Research Corp. Determined. 1978. $18-25. Not
shown: Lucy, Charlie Brown, Woodstock. Each
puppet was sold individually

Cotton fold up puppet and bottle holder from
Knickerbocker. 1980s. $5-10

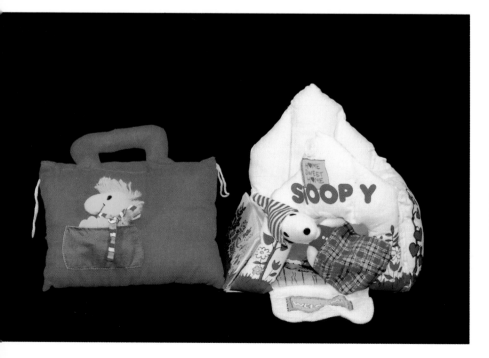

Soft cotton Snoopy (separate) inside cotton
stuffed doghouse. Woodstock and Snoopy can
be played with separately. Knickerbocker.
1980s. $20-30

Plush sitting Snoopy. (Red tag should be around neck). Determined. 1971. This was made in a 12" and 15" size. $15-35

Plush Woodstock puppet from Applause. Mid-1990s. $25-35

Plush Snoopy puppet, Paw Pets, Applause. 1990s. $20-30

Plush and denim Learning Snoopy from Knickerbocker. 1980s. $20-25

35th Anniversary special edition Snoopy, bag included.
Determined productions. 1985. $125-150

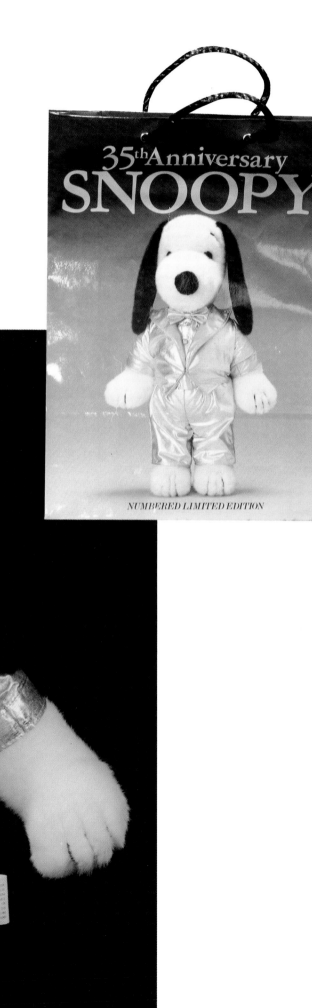

Plush "Boy George" (singer from Culture Club) Snoopy by Determined. His legs are still and he stands alone. Early 1980s. $40-60. Not shown is Mr. T (from the A team) Snoopy. 1980s. Determined. $40-60

Plush Joe Cool toy. Special limited edition with certificate. Determined. 1980s. $80-100

Plush #1 racing Snoopy from Applause. 1990s. $18-25

Plush Santa Snoopy. Determined. Plush Snoopys were produced widely from 1968-1980s and this makes them hard to date and not extremely valuable. They came in 12" and 18". Clothing was made and sold separately or outfitted as something special, such as Santa Snoopy. $20-30

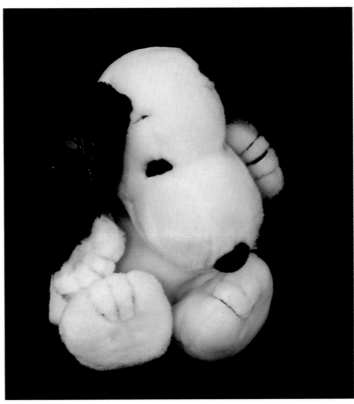

Plush Snoopy puppet from Applause. Mid-1990s. $20-30

Plush graduate Snoopy toy from Applause.
Mid-1990s. $20-25

"Earresistible" Snoopy by Applause. Wire in
ears for posing. 1990s. $18-25

Plush Snoopy from Macy's. Also came with
Macy's scarf. 1980s. $40-60

Plush Snoopy reindeer from Camp Snoopy.
1994. $20-30.

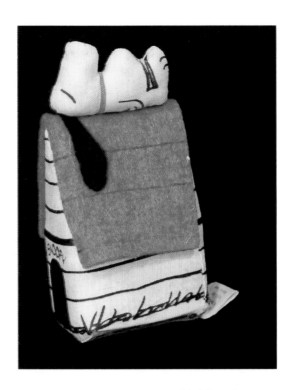

Cotton Snoopy on doghouse with felt roof. Hallmark. 1970s. $5-7

Cotton Autograph graduate Snoopy. Applause. 1990s. $20-30

Cloth Snoopy Autograph Doghouse. 1984. Determined Productions. $25-30

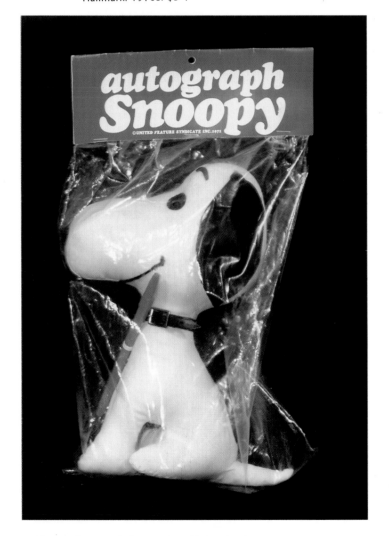

Cotton Autograph Snoopy from Determined. 10.5". $25-35

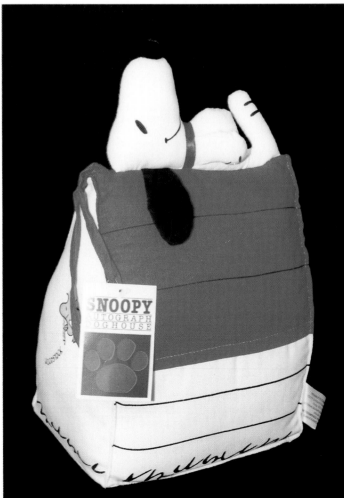

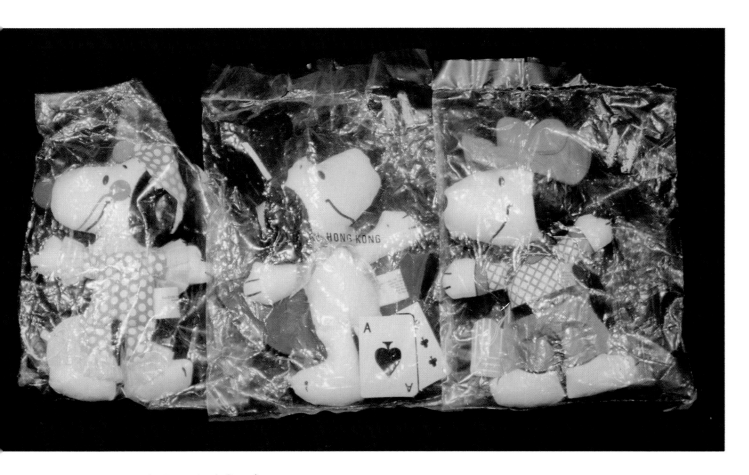

Cloth, stuffed Snoopys by Determined. Came in
a variety of costumes. 1980s. $10-20 ea.

Cloth Snoopys by Determined. 1980s. Average
height 6". 1980s. $10-20 each

Box with cloth Snoopy by Applause. 1990. $7-10

Cotton stuffed Snoopy on roller skates by Determined. 1980s. $6-10.

Box with cloth Snoopy by Applause. 1990. $7-10

Plush baby Snoopy laying down, baby toy. Also came without rattle . 1980s-1990s. Applause and Determined produced these. $7-10

Baby plush Snoopy with rattle inside. Also came in blue. Determined. Late 1980s. $30-40

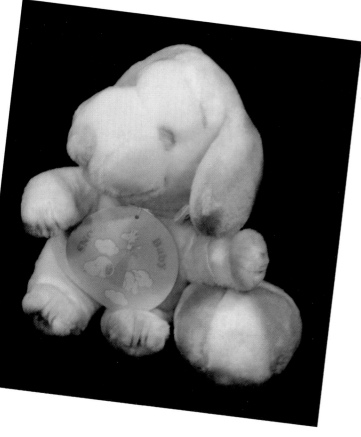

Plush baby Snoopy with blue ears and paws with plush ball. Determined. 1980s. $30-40

Plush Snoopy toy. Applause. 1990s. $25-35

Plush baby Snoopy toy. Applause. 1990s. $25-35

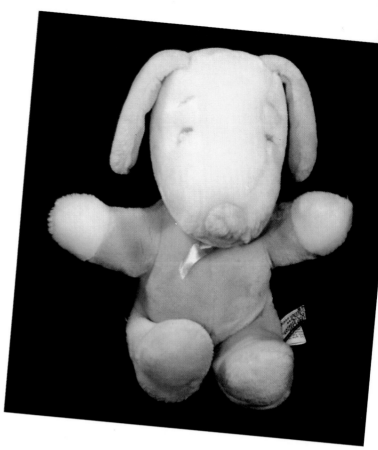

Plush blue Snoopy. Late 1980s. Also came in pink. Determined. $30-40

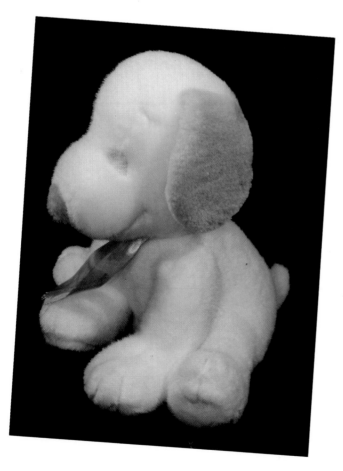

Plush baby musical Snoopy with blue ears. Determined. 1980s. Head moves as music plays. $50-75

Plush Snoopy hand muff. Determined. Early 1980s. $25-35

Cotton rag doll Snoopy in jeans and Peanuts Gang tee shirt. Ideal and Determined made this same doll; only the box was different. 14". 1970s. $15-20

Plush Snoopy fanny pack. Applause. 1990s.
$20-30

Cotton Snoopy in Snoopy shirt from Determined. 1980s. 8". $10-20

Plush stuffed orange Snoopy. 1980s.
Determined. $10-15

Plush blue standing Snoopy. 1980s.
Determined. Came in a variety of bold
colors. $10-15

Gift pack. Book, cotton Snoopy, carrying case.
Applause. Late 1980s. $15-20

Gift pack. Book, cotton Snoopy, carrying case.
Applause. Late 1980s. $15-20

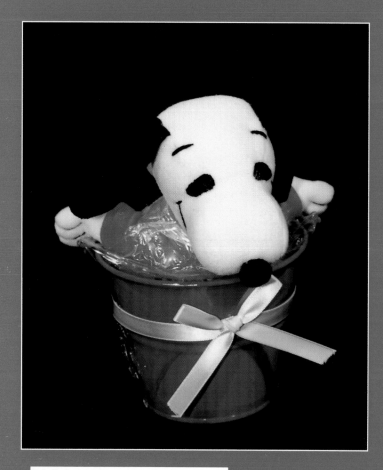

Stuffed plush Snoopy in bucket gift set. Applause. Early 1990s. $20-30

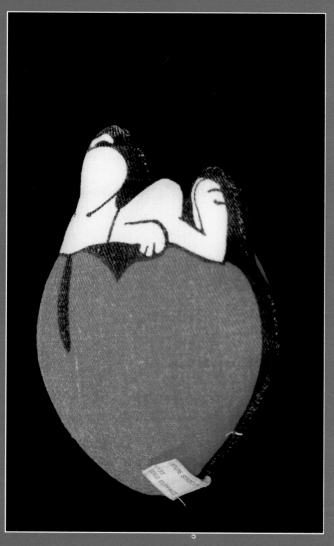

Cotton fabric heart shaped Snoopy car deodorizer. 1980s. $4-6.

Snoopy's wardrobe. Yellow raincoat. Determined. 1970s. Came in 12" and 18". $20-30

Nylon jogging shirt, pants were included.
Determined. 1970s. Came in 11" and 17".
$20-30

Snoopy accessories set. Tennis visor and shoes.
Late 1970s. Determined. 12", $7-10; 18",
$10-15

SNOOPY'S BABYWORLD

Checkered bank and Snoopy block bank.
Determined Productions. Mid-1970s. $25-35

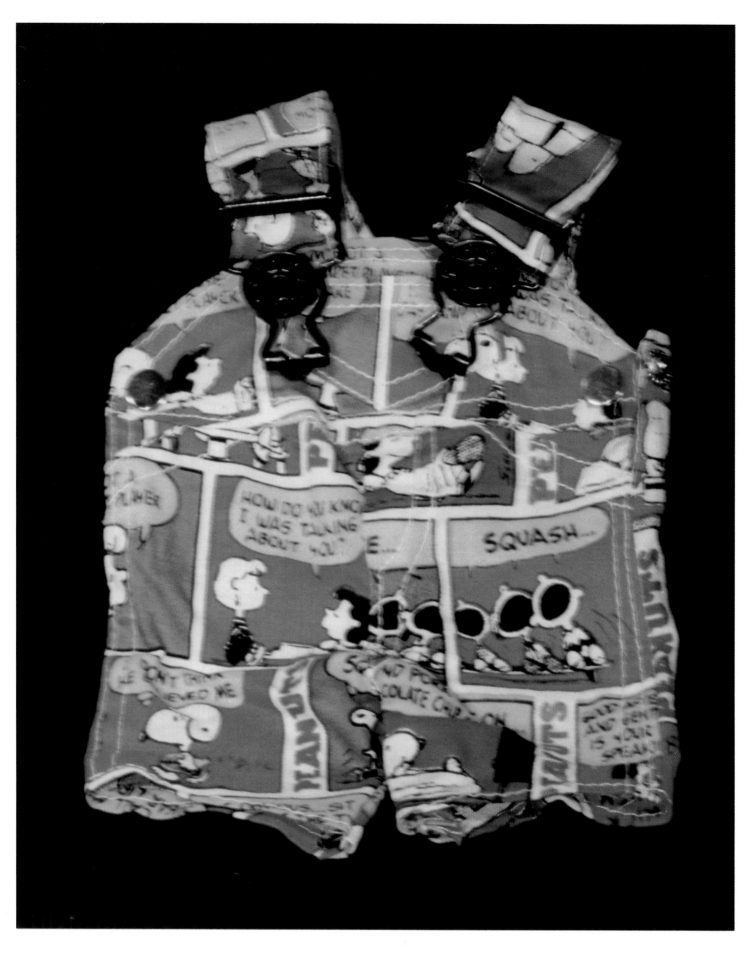

Snoopy fun overalls. Determined. 12" and 18"
$15-20

Silverplated 40th anniversary Snoopy baby
place setting by Goedinger. 1990. $30-40

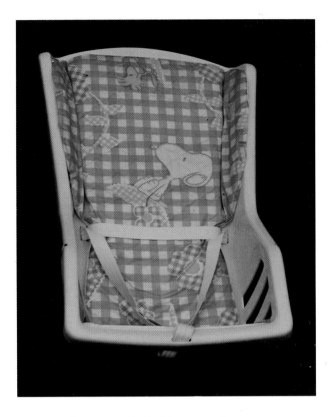

Plastic infant seat with vinyl Snoopy pad.
Questor Corp. 1970s. $15-20

Kol Kraft vinyl Rock-A-Bye Baby Carrier. 1980s. $30-40

Silverplated 40th anniversary baby cup with
Snoopy on the handle. Goedinger. 1990.
$15-20

Baby car seat and liner by Kolcraft. Late 1980s.
$40-50

Plastic Snoopy divided baby dish. Danara.
1980s-1990s. $7-10

Plastic Snoopy cup. By Danara. 1980s. Missing
lid. $4-6

Vinyl baby splash mat. Danara. 4" x 5". 1990s.
$11-16

Snoopy and Woodstock silver fork. Danara.
1980s-1990s. $4-5

Snoopy and Woodstock baby feeding spoon
plastic bowl with. Danara. 1980s-1990s. $4-5

Snoopy and Woodstock silver spoon. Danara.
1980s-1990s. $4-5

Silver baby spoon. Snoopy and Woodstock
standing. on ball. Danara. 1980s-1990s. $4-5

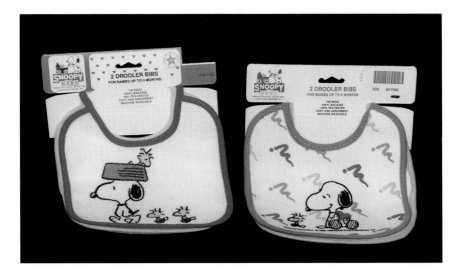

Cotton bib set. Danara. 1980-1990s. $3-4

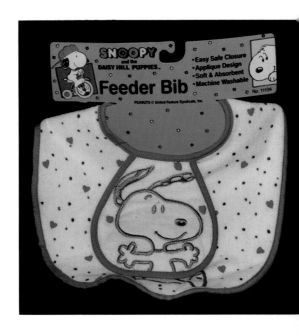

Plastic napkin clip. Makes napkin into bib. Pecoware. 1990s. $5-7

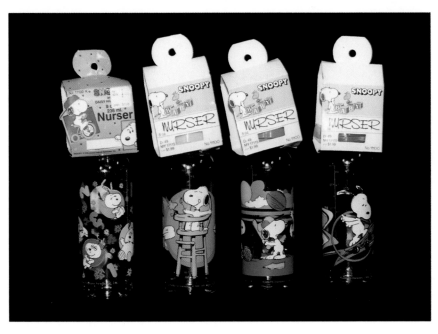

Plastic nurser bottles. Danara. 1990s. 4oz and 6oz. $4-6

Baby nail clippers by Danara. 1990s. $2-3

Cotton bib set. Danara-Delux. 1995. $7-9

Plastic brush sets. Danara. 1980-1990s. $3-4

Baby pacifier by Danara. 1990s. $3-5

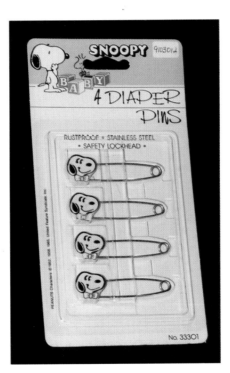

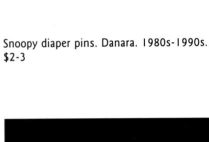

Snoopy diaper pins. Danara. 1980s-1990s. $2-3

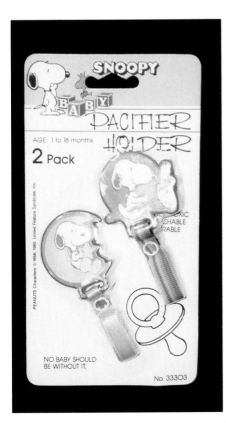

Romper Room plastic baby toy with bell. 1980s. $5-7

Snoopy pacifier holder. Mid-1990s. Danara. $3-4

Plastic juice box bottles. Danara. Mid-1990s.
$3-4

Plastic musical crib exerciser plays "It's a small
world." 1980s. $20-25

Plastic copter. Busy Box crib toy. Early 1980s.
Hasbro/Romper Room. $25-35

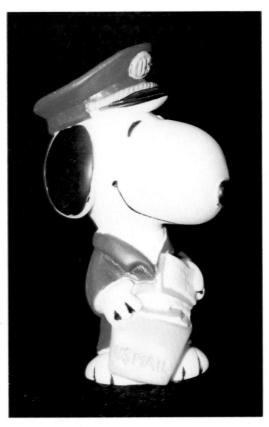

Vinyl baby toy, Snoopy Postman. Late 1980s.
$5-8

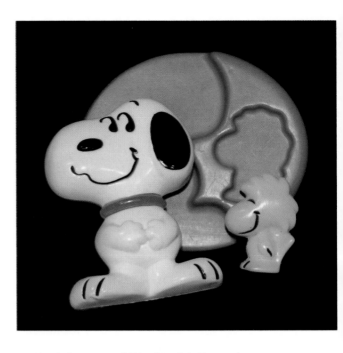

Plastic Snoopy and Woodstock bath puzzle.
Danara. 1980s. $5-8

Inflatable jingling toy bubble by Remco. 1990s.
$2-3

Vinyl inflatable water spout cover for bathtub.
Danara. Mid-1990s. $6-8

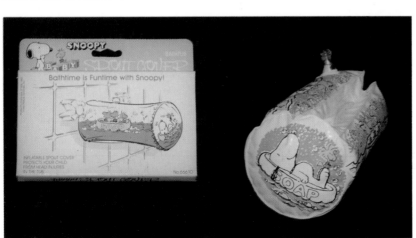

Plastic inflatable baby rattle by Remco. 1990s.
Came in many colors and pictures. $2-3

Inflatable baby bop bags. Came in many colors.
1990s. $2-3

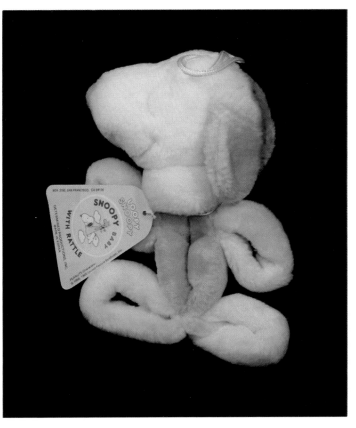

Plush Snoopy baby toy with rattle. Determined. Early 1980s. $15-20

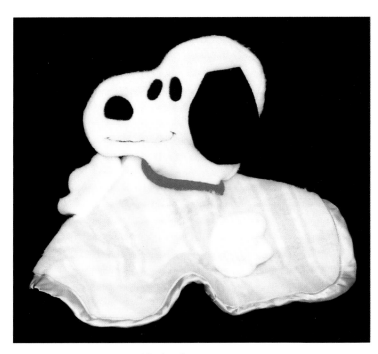

Acrylic Snoopy Snuggli blanket from
Knickerbocker. 1980s. $5-10.

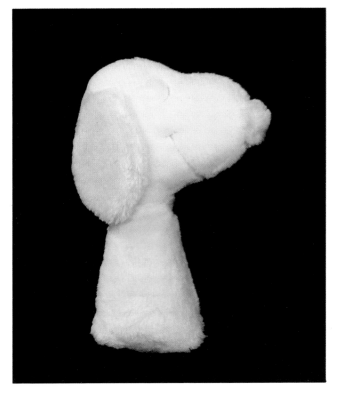

Plush Snoopy with blue ears, rattle. Late
1980s. Determined. $10-15

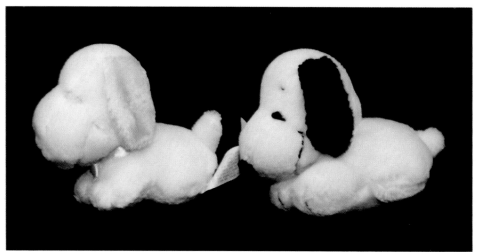

Plush baby Snoopys. Black ears and blue ears. Pink not shown. Came with and without rattle inside. Determined and Applause made these. $5-7 each

Plush Beagle mobile with squeaker. Determined. 1980s. $20-30

Sports vinyl diaper bag. 1990s. $20-25

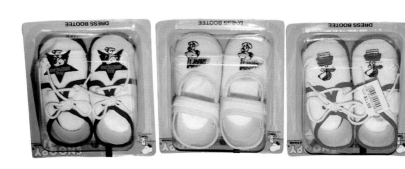

Baby booties. 1980s. $4-6

Vinyl diaper bag. 1990s. $10-15

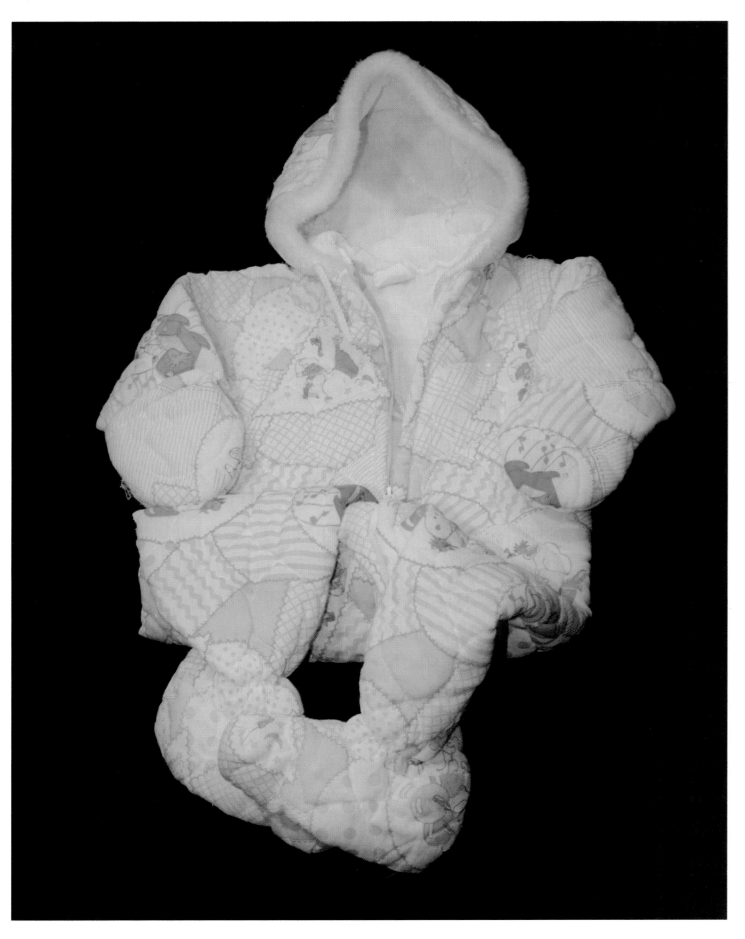

Cotton/polyester baby bunting from Sears. 1980s. $10-20

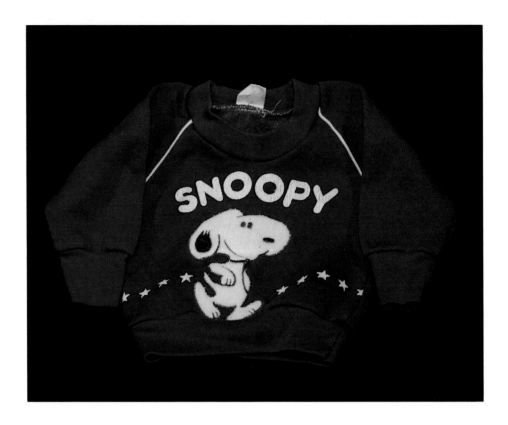

Cotton child's Snoopy sweat shirt. 1980s. $6-8

Cotton infant's Snoopy tee shirt. 1980s. $4-6

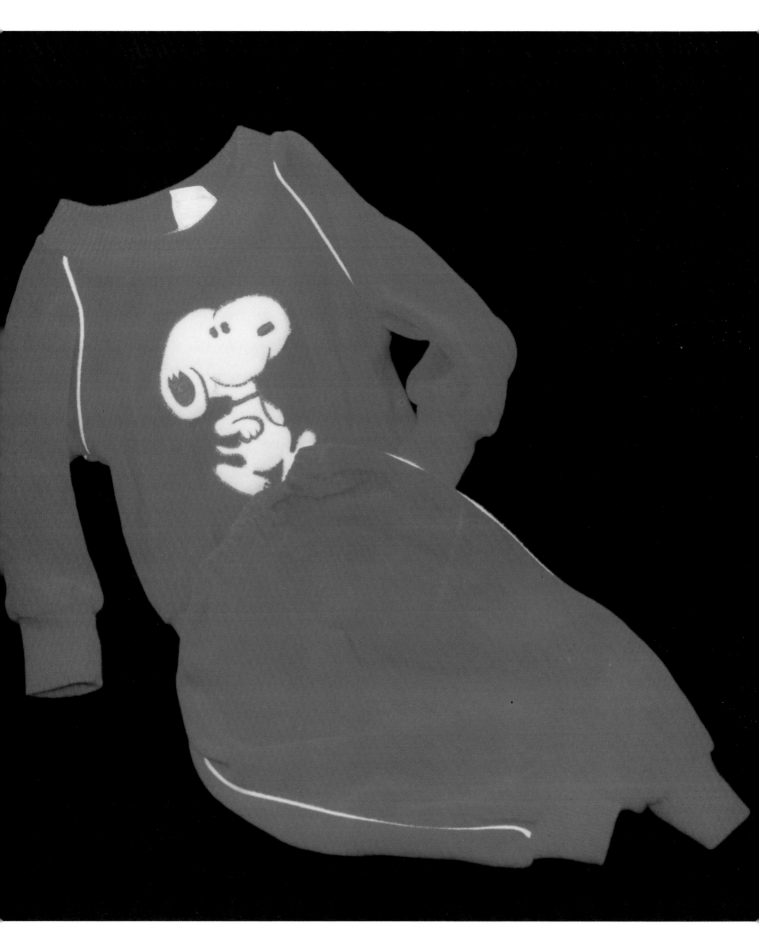

Velour Babyfair infant's two-piece suit. 1980s.
$15-20

Cotton child's tee shirt. 1980s. $5-7

Cotton child's Snoopy sweat shirt. 1990s.
$9-12

Cotton Snoopy child's sweat shirt 1990s. $6-8

Cotton Snoopy child's sweat shirt. 1980s. $5-7

Cotton child's sweat shirt. 1980s. $5-7

Cotton child's two piece suit. Came with tricot Snoopy toy. 1990s. $15-20

Cotton Peanuts girl's Snoopy tee shirt. 1990s. $12-15 new

Cotton Peanuts girl's Snoopy tee shirt. 1990s. $12-15 new

Cotton Snoopy child's tee shirt. 1990s. $5-8

Cotton children's tee shirt. 1990s. $5-7

Acrylic child's knit Snoopy hat. 1980s. $5-7

Cotton children's Snoopy cap. Peanuts. Mid-1990s. $5-7

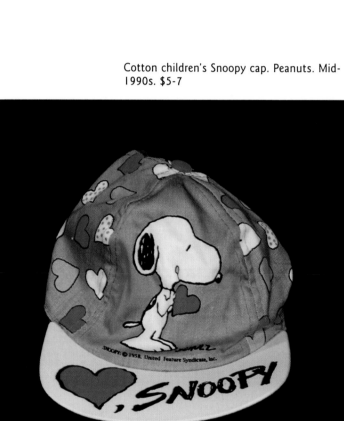

Cotton baby hat. 1996. Came with baby outfit. $2-3

Cotton children's Snoopy cap. Peanuts. Mid-1990s. $5-7

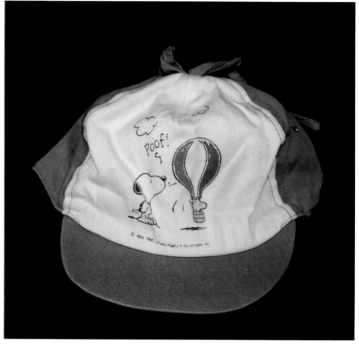

Hard back Snoopy books. American Education Publishing. Mid-1990s. $3-5

Cotton children's Snoopy cap. 1980s. $5-7

Cotton Snoopy wall hanging. Filgo,
early 1980s. $20-30

Cotton Snoopy with balloons and Woodstock
wall hanging. 1990s. $40-50

Snoopy pellon wall hanging. 1980s. $15-20

Cotton pajama bag. Nighttime Snoopy. 1980s.
$10-15

Doghouse with Snoopy, wall hanging. Silgo.
Early 1990s. 32" x 34". $60-70

Cotton hanging shoe bag. 1980s. $10-15

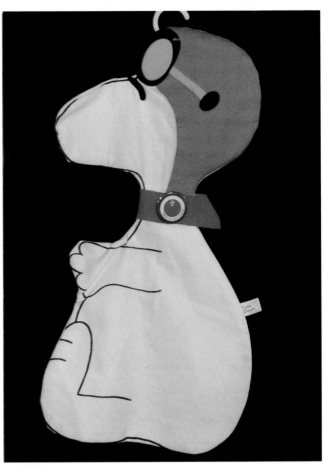

Cotton with felt Flying Ace pajama bag. Simon Simple. 1970s. $25-30

Felt Snoopy and Woodstock pajama case from Simon Simple. Early 1970s. $25-30

Plush, sleeping Snoopy, pajama bag by Determined Productions. 1970s. $15-25

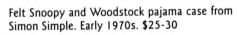

Cotton Snoopy with felt trim on doghouse pajama bag. Simon Simple. 1970s. $25-30

Cotton Flying Ace pajama bag with felt trim. Simon Simple. 1970s. $25-30

Fabric hanging shoe bag. 1980s. $10-15

Fabric hanging shoe bag. 1980s. $10-15

Ceramic Snoopy bank. Determined. 1969. Made in Italy, hand painted, artistic, heavy ceramic, in two sizes. 6" and 8.5". Shown: 6"; $40-50; 8.5" 40-60 (not shown). Not shown: Charlie Brown, 8.5", $60-75; Charlie Brown, 6", 50-60; Linus, 8.5", $65-80; Linus, 6", $40-60; Lucy, 8.5", $75-100; Lucy, 6", $50-60

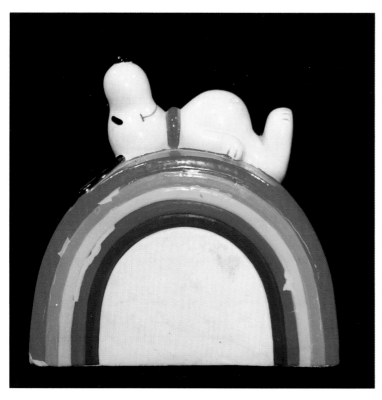

Papier mache Snoopy on rainbow bank.
Determined. 1976. $18-22

Papier mache Snoopy on dog house bank.
Determined. 1970s. Very common. $5-7

Papier mache Belle bank. Determined. 1981.
$15-25

Ceramic Snoopy in football helmet bank.
Determined. 1979. $15-20. Not shown in this
series: Snoopy in tennis visor, in top hat and
tux, in yellow rain slicker, in grey hard hat, or
in red baseball hat. $20-30 each.

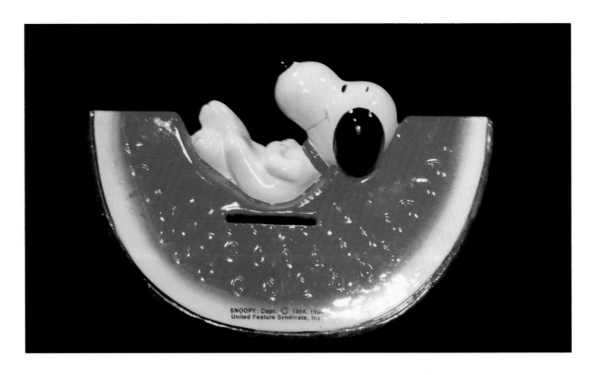

Papier mache Snoopy on melon bank from the
fruit series. Determined. 1976. $25-35

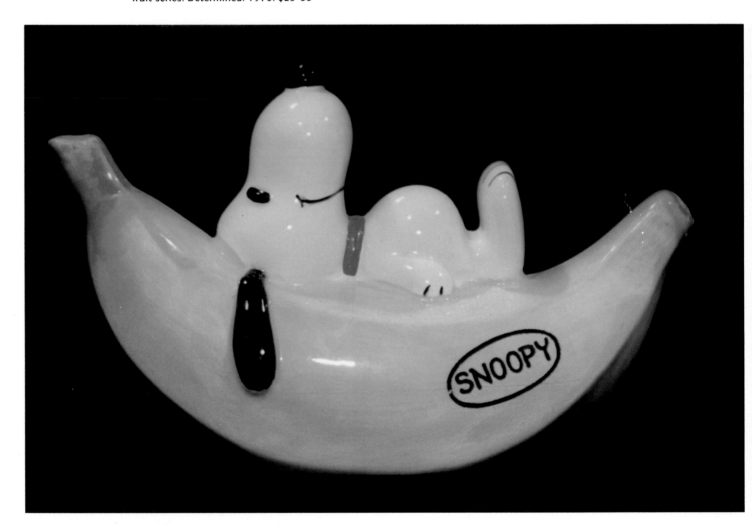

Papier mache Snoopy laying on banana bank.
Determined. 1976. $15-20. Not shown: apple,
strawberry, orange, $30-40; lemon with
Woodstock, $25-35

Papier mache Snoopy on soccer ball bank from the sports series. Determined. 1976. $20-25

Snoopy in french fry box, ceramic bank. Junk food series banks from Determined. 1979. Not shown in series: Snoopy on hamburger, Snoopy on hot dog, Snoopy in front of chocolate ice cream cone. $40-50 each

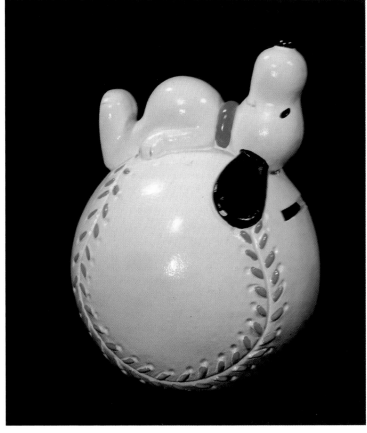

Papier mache Snoopy on baseball bank. Determined. 1976. $20-25. Not shown in this series: basketball, $20-25; football, $22-30; bowling ball, $30-40

Egg-shaped ceramic Cool cash bank. Willitts.
Late 1980s. $20-25

Tin globe shaped Snoopy bank. Ohio Art.
1980s. $10-15

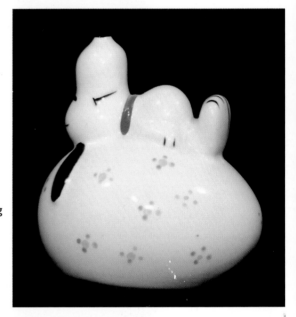

Ceramic Snoopy on egg
bank. Determined
Productions. 1970s.
$25-35

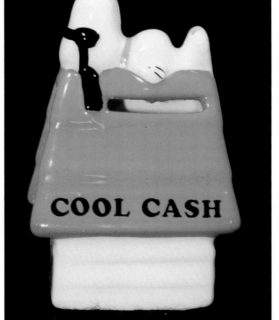

Snoopy on Cool cash doghouse ceramic bank.
Willitts. Roof came in a variety of colors. Late
1980s. $20-25

Plastic German Snoopy jumping hurdle. "Du nimmst jede hurde." 1990s. $20-25

Plastic bank Snoopy sitting on dog house in suit, Joe Banker. Applause. 1990. $20-27

Snoopy ceramic train engine bank. Willitts. 1990. $35-45

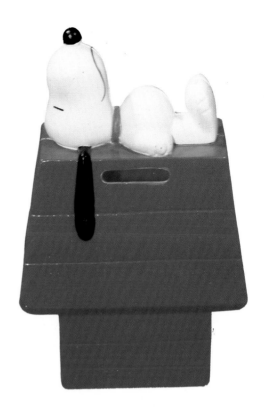

Plastic doghouse bank. Promotion for Chex Mix. 1990s. $8-12

Tin 40th Anniversary bank. Japan. 1990.
$15-25

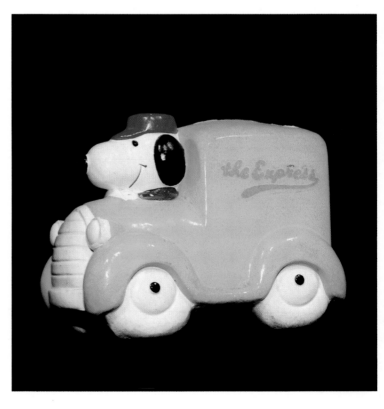

Papier mache yellow truck bank. "The Express" bank. Determined Productions. 1977. $25-35. Others not shown: Snoopy in red convertible; Snoopy in motorboat; Snoopy in green truck; Snoopy in blue convertible. $25-35 each

Ceramic Snoopy Christmas planter. 1970s. Also
came with a red hat. $60-75

Ceramic planter by Determined Productions.
Mid-1970s. 7.5" $40-50. (Not shown: 4.5", $25-
35)

Ceramic planter shaped like an open book.
Determined. Mid-1970s. $35-45

Octagonal Ceramic planter. Determined.
Snoopy and Woodstock on alternate sides. Mid-
1970s. 2.25" x 4.5". $25-35

Ceramic drum shaped planter. Determined.
Mid-1970s. $30-40

Plastic doghouse planter with plush Snoopy
sitting on top. Telafloral planter/Valentines gift
with flowers. Early 1990s. $15-25

Ceramic candle holder. "Everyone looks better
by candlelight." Hallmark. Mid-1970s. 2.5".
$20-25

Ceramic candle holder. "Snoopy-Bleah!"
Hallmark. Mid-1970s. 3". $20-25

Christmas Snoopy pillar candle from Hallmark.
Mid-1970s. 6". $15-20

Candle with Snoopy holding Woodstock. Hallmark. 1990s. $5-7

Happy day candle. Hallmark. 1980s-1990s. $4-6

Candle with Snoopy on doghouse. Hallmark. 1990s. $5-7

Tin Halloween bucket with candle inside. Willitts. 1990s. $15-20

Plastic love light votive cups with box. Made in Holland. Dick de Rijk Productions. Late 1980s. $6-10

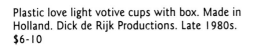

Ceramic plate. Tribute to the art of Charles Schulz. Mall of America, Bloomington, Mn. 1994. $20-30

Ceramic plate. "40 Years of Happiness." 1990. $30-40 with box

Ceramic "Dear Mom" bell. Schmid. 1979.
$25-35

Ceramic Bi-Centennial plate. 1776-1976.
Schmid. $35-45 with box.

Ceramic Mothers Day plate. 1988. Willitts.
$25-30 with box

Ceramic Christmas plate. 1990. Willitts.
$25-30 with box

Ceramic Christmas plate. 1981. Schmid.
$25-30 with box

Ceramic Mothers Day plate. 1979. Schmid.
$25-30 with box

Ceramic Valentine's Day plate. 1977. Schmid.
$25-30 with box

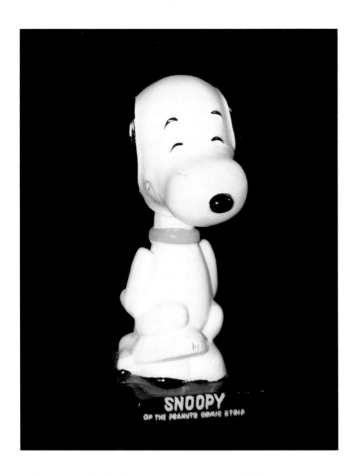

Snoopy nodder by Determined. 1959. Lego. 5.5".
$50-100

Papier mache figurine from Determined. $25-35

Papier mache figurine by Determined Productions. Early 1970s. 5.5". $30-40

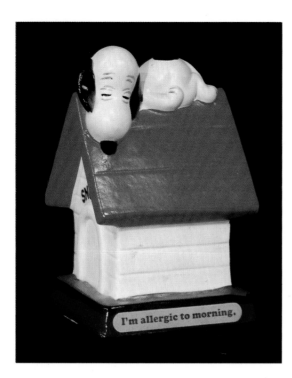

Snoopy on dog house, "I'm allergic to morning."
4.25". $30-35. Came in 17 other various
figurines of all characters, not shown.

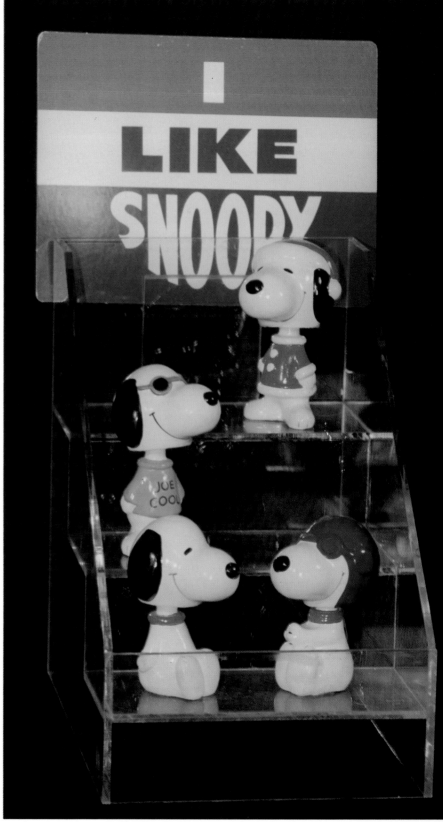

Bobbing head papier mache Snoopys. Determined. 1976. 4". $25-50 each

Flying ace paper mache bobbing head figurine
by Determined Productions. 1976. $25-50

Joe Cool bobbing head figurine by Determined
Productions. 1976. $25-50

Bobbing head figurine by Determined Productions. 4". 1976. $25-35. Not shown: Woodstock,
Lucy, Charlie Brown. $25-50 each

Bobbing head Santa Snoopy. Determined. 1976.
$25-50

Metal Snoopy balancing set. Japan. 1990s.
$35-50

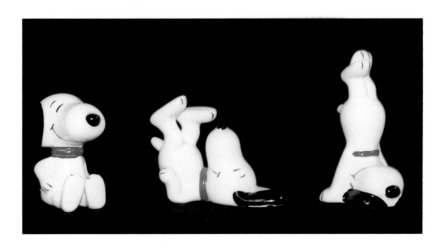

Ceramic Snoopy in different poses. Determined.
1980s. $15-20 each

Ceramic heart shaped dish with Snoopy on lid.
1980s. Determined. $20-30

Ceramic Snoopy figurine, 1980s. $10-15

Willitts Snoopy sports porcelain ornaments.
1980s. $20-30 each

Miniature porcelain Snoopy figurine. 2". 1990.
Willitts. This was part of a series in of the
Peanuts gang in party attire. $20-30

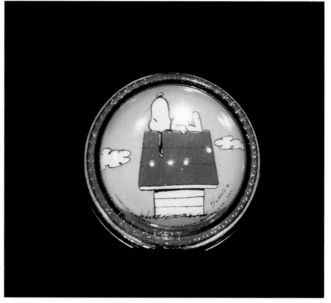

Snoopy laying on doghouse glass dome
paperweight. Butterfly. 1970s. $25-35.

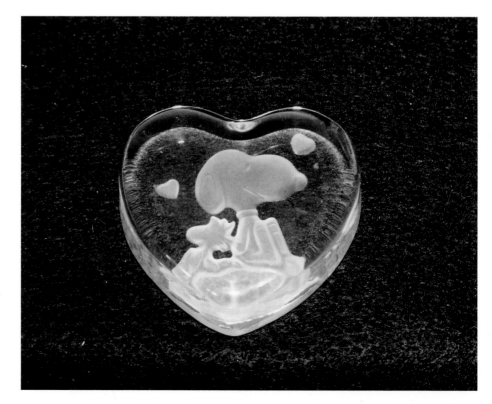

Etched glass heart paperweight by Butterfly. 3"
x 2.5 ". 1979. $50-75 in box. Also available but
not shown: Heart with Snoopy sniffing flowers,
1979, 3" x 2.5", $50-75; Glass heart with
Snoopy and friends, 1979, $50-75; Round glass
Snoopy with football done with paper picture
underneath, 1970s, $25-35; Round glass
Snoopy tennis dome, 1970s, $25-35.

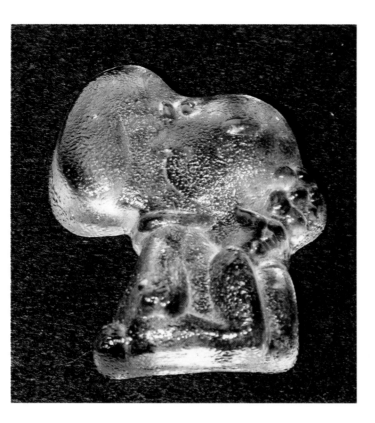

Glass stipple-etched Snoopy with flower paperweight by Determined, 1970s. 4.5" x 3.5". $35-45. Not shown: Woodstock, 2.5" x 3", $30-40

Ceramic egg from Aviva. 1970s. 3". $15-20

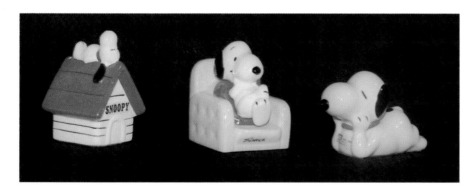

Ceramic Snoopy paperweights. Mid- and late 1970s. Butterfly. $15-30 each

Ceramic Snoopy paperweights Mid- and late 1970s. Butterfly. $15-30 each

Ceramic Snoopy paperweights. Late 1970s. Butterfly. $15-30 each

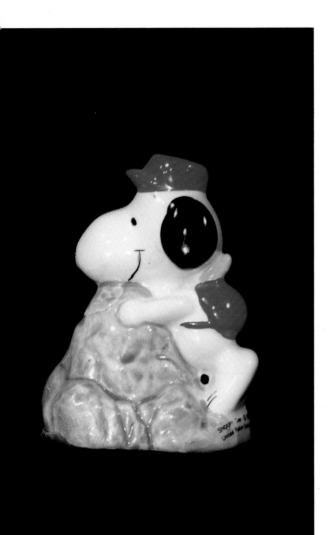

Ceramic Snoopy climbing mountain paperweight. Determined. 1980s. $25-35

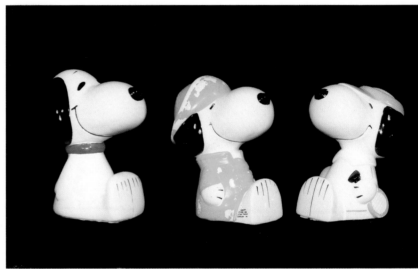

Sitting Snoopy ceramic paperweights. Butterfly. 1979. $15-20 each

Ceramic Snoopy paperweights. Mid- and late 1970s. Butterfly. $15-30 each

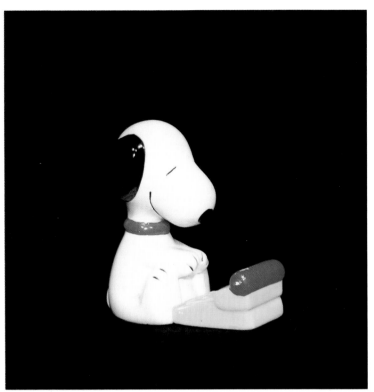

Ceramic mini Snoopy at typewriter paperweight from Butterfly. Early 1970s. $10-15

Snoopy and Woodstock on ceramic base, mini-
paperweight from Butterfly. 1970s. $10-15.

Ceramic Snoopy leaning on green base mini
paperweight. 1.5". Butterfly. 1980s. $10-15.

Snoopy in red hat on ceramic black base, mini-
paperweight from Butterfly. 1970s. $10-15

Snoopy ceramic pencil/pen holders. Mid-1970s. Butterfly. $25-35

Snoopy ceramic mini-paperweights. Early 1980s. $7-12 each

Snoopy mini-paperweight. Butterfly. 1980s. $7-12

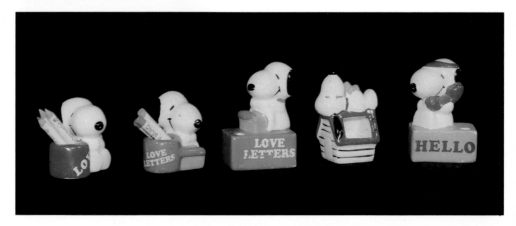

Ceramic Pencil holders. 5 different poses. Butterfly. 1980s. $7-12

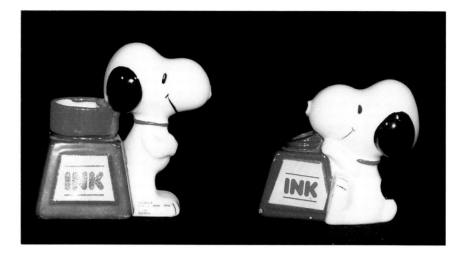

Snoopy ceramic ink wells. Butterfly. Mid-1970s. 3.5" x 4". $25-35

Ceramic pencil holders. Butterfly. Mid-1970s. $25-35

Ceramic pen holders. 1970s. Butterfly. $20-30 each

Ceramic pencil holders for mini pencils with Snoopy posing. Butterfly. 1980s. $7-12

BIBLIOGRAPHY

Rheta Grinslay Johnson. *"Good Grief:" The Story of Charles Schulz*. New York: Pharos Books, 1989.

Jim Fanning. In *Boomer Magazine*. Dubuque, Iowa: Antique Trader Publications, April, 1995.

Charles M. Holt. *You Don't Look 35 Charlie Brown*. New York: Holt, Rhinehart, Winston, 1985.